# School Behaviour and Families

Frameworks for working together

Edited by

## Sue Roffey

**David Fulton Publishers**
London

**This book is dedicated with love and thanks to my own parents, Anne and Harry Downs.**

David Fulton Publishers Ltd
Ormond House, 26–27 Boswell Street, London WC1N 3JZ

www.fultonpublishers.co.uk

First published in Great Britain in 2002 by David Fulton Publishers

Copyright © 2002 David Fulton Publishers

*British Library Cataloguing in Publication Data*
A catalogue record for this book is available from the British Library.

ISBN 1 85346 776 6

Typeset by Servis Filmsetting Ltd, Manchester
Printed and bound in Great Britain by The Cromwell Press, Trowbridge, Wilts.

# Contents

# Acknowledgements

I owe a debt of gratitude to all the participants in the research study but especially the parents/carers who agreed to be interviewed. It was not always easy for parents to tell their stories and I appreciate the courage it must have taken and the confidence invested in me. I hope that I have represented their views and concerns fully.

I would like to thank all those who helped with the research process, with a special mention to Susan Davies.

I was immensely fortunate to have two of the leading commentators on the issues as my research supervisor and external research consultant. Sheila Wolfendale at the University of East London is renowned for her work with parents and schools, and Emilia Dowling at the Tavistock Clinic for the joint systems approach to problems with children. My thanks go to both of these exceptional women for their valuable support and guidance.

I am grateful to all those colleagues who shared my commitment to this project, especially those who agreed to contribute as fellow authors despite their own heavy work loads and/or personal commitments.

My thanks to those who read some or all of the manuscript and made valuable comments, especially Dominic Boddington, Terry O'Reirdan and Sarah Lovesy, all working as teachers in England or Australia.

It's a pleasure working with David Fulton Publishers. They are efficient, helpful and non-intrusive. A special thanks to commissioning editor Jude Bowen.

Finally, this book would not exist if it were not for the unfailing support of my family, especially my partner David. My love and thanks as ever.

# Foreword

I was delighted to be asked to write this Foreword. Upon receiving a set of proofs, I at once became absorbed in the whole book. It offers a distinctive and fresh outlook upon an area of home–school relations that has received scant attention – namely issues of 'behaviour' and how teachers and parents/carers construe, define and respond to problematic challenging.

We know, as professionals and parents, how teacher–parent relationships can often be fraught and imbued with apparently irreconcilable views and attributions held by all parties, often to the detriment of the children whose interests parents and teachers have at heart.

The book's authors seek to explore and challenge such stereotypes and offer models and solutions to facilitate working links in the spirit of partnership, as espoused and encouraged in the revised SEN Code of Practice, the publication of which, at the end of 2001, fortuitously predates that of this book by a matter of months.

Sue Roffey and the other chapter writers have assembled a judicious mix of perspectives upon problematic behaviour. Sue herself, as editor and lead author, vividly presents the parental voice and, from her research, proposes a core working model (Chapter 6) characterised as a 'plugged-in interface'. This metaphor graphically portrays connections between home and school and the model is proposed as a theory–practice framework that lends itself to practical application by teachers and parents/carers.

Uniquely, there are four chapters that address children's situations that, historically, schools have found rather challenging, that is, how to sensitively and appropriately meet the needs of children from abusing homes, who live a mobile life-style, who are in public care and who are from 'diverse' communities. The issues raised and solutions offered in Chapters 7, 8, 9, 10 and 11 are done so in acknowledgement that responsibilities in fostering partnership are corporate – all partners have a part to play in safeguarding children's well-being.

Sue and her colleagues are to be congratulated for sharing their practice and their ideas with a wide audience.

I welcome this book as a valuable contribution to the growing library on home–school links.

Sheila Wolfendale
January 2002

# About the Authors

**Elizabeth Gillies** has worked as a teacher and educational psychologist. She presently works as a consultant psychologist with international schools and their communities in Japan. She was a senior educational psychologist in Surrey for four years before leaving the UK. Elizabeth's particular interest is in developing psychological conversations mainly using solution focused thinking.

**Anna Harskamp** is an educational psychologist who has also worked as a teacher and as a nursing assistant. For over 20 years she has worked in East London, with teachers and school staff, children and families. Her particular areas of interest are in child protection, trauma and loss. Anna is currently Principal Educational Psychologist/Assistant Head of Children's Support in the London Borough of Barking and Dagenham.

**Jean Law** is a senior educational psychologist in Essex where she has a responsibility for behaviour in schools. Her work has brought her into contact with many families in difficulty and children in public care. Jean is co-author of the Essex Schools Award Scheme which promotes and acknowledges good practice in the development of whole-school approaches.

**Ann Phoenix** is a senior lecturer in psychology at the Open University. Her research interests include motherhood and social identities including those of race, ethnicity and gender. She has written widely on related issues, including young people's experiences of racism. Ann's current research is on the construction of identities in young people.

**Sue Roffey** was a teacher in both mainstream schools and specialist provision for students with behavioural difficulties. She became an educational psychologist in 1987 and now specialises in emotional, social and behavioural issues in education. Sue is currently attached to the University of Western Sydney and works as a trainer and independent consultant in Australia and the UK.

**Anthea Wormington** has taught in both primary and secondary schools as a teacher of English/drama and special educational needs. She has been involved in Traveller education for 20 years and has been the Coordinator of Traveller Education in the London Borough of Newham for 10 years.

Sue Roffey has many years' experience as a teacher and an educational psychologist. She is currently based in Australia where she is attached to the University of Western Sydney. Sue works as a researcher and consultant on emotional, social and behavioural issues in education and has written widely on these topics. She is a founder member of ESIA, a network promoting emotional literacy in Australia.

Sue provides professional development and training in both Australia and the UK. She can be contacted at sue@sueroffey.com

# CHAPTER 1

# Introduction

Although parental involvement has swept through the educational landscape
. . . the area of problem behaviour in schools has been almost totally neglected
and the question of how to work positively and productively with parents in
such circumstances remains largely unanswered.                    (Miller 1994)

Imagine this: It is the second week of the new school year. Year 4 teacher
Norma McFarlane stops Liam's mum, Penny, as she walks out of the classroom door at the end of the day. 'Would you be able to have a word with
me tomorrow after school?' Penny's shoulders droop, she glances around
to make sure other parents have left and then nods grimly towards her
son: 'Is he getting up to his old tricks again?' She becomes defensive: 'I
really don't think there's any point me coming here again; I told the last
teacher, he's no problem at home.' Mrs McFarlane smiles and says: 'He's
getting on really well; I want to make sure it continues. I need your help
in telling me a bit more about him and what works for you.' The next day
Penny turns up to hear the good news in more detail. It makes a change
from hearing about all the terrible things her son has done. She listens to
Mrs McFarlane's plans to reward Liam for certain behaviours in the classroom. The teacher then asks if Penny has any ideas herself. By the end
of 20 minutes they have agreed on a plan. Both teacher and parent decide
to talk again every week to see how it's going. Penny walks out of the
school feeling that this teacher actually likes her son despite his difficulties and that, as his mother, she can hold her head high again. Someone
wanted to know, and took account of, what she had to say and what she
had to offer.

  Now imagine this: Dee comes into the staff room, pours some tea and
plumps herself down next to Alice. She sighs: 'I'm going to have to get Mrs
Fitzgerald up here again.' Alice raises an eyebrow: 'Kylie still giving you
trouble then?' Dee throws up her hands in exasperation. 'She won't settle

to work, she's always getting in the way of the others, she kicked Michael this morning and her language . . .' There's no need to go on. Alice shrugs. 'But with her background what can you expect . . . all the Fitzgerald children have been difficult one way or another. Mum has no idea how to control them and I don't think there's been a man on the scene since the boyfriend walked out last year.' Dee continues: 'The last time I had Mrs Fitzgerald up here she was 30 minutes late, had a little one in tow who disrupted the interview and then she never did the things she promised – like making sure Kylie did her homework and getting her to school on time. I don't know why I bother.' Alice nods in sympathy and the bell rings for end of playtime.

Although the individuals in these anecdotes are fictional, the stories are based on a number of observed events. Elements in them reflect different realities in schools and it would be surprising if readers did not recognise similar conversations. Both stories illustrate some of the issues that are addressed in this book:

- concern about behaviour in school
- attributions for behaviour
- expectations about parental involvement and 'partnership'
- the processes by which parents may become involved
- the context for parents
- the influence of school culture.

A central theme of *School Behaviour and Families* is that working in collaboration with parents and carers may provide the best chance of success for addressing behavioural difficulties in school. In Britain the *Special Educational Needs Code of Practice* is unequivocal about the importance of parental involvement:

> There are strong reasons for working in partnership with parents. If they feel confident that schools and professionals actively involve them, take account of their wishes, feelings and unique perspectives on their children's development, then the work of those schools and professionals can be more effective. This is particularly so if a child has special needs.
>
> (DfEE 2000: 8)

But what does 'working in collaboration' mean and what are parents' perspectives on this? Parents and teachers do not necessarily see things the same way and there is evidence that teachers' views often take precedence within home–school discussions (e.g. MacLure and Walker 1999). It is therefore not surprising that relationships break down and stereotypes are strengthened.

## Definition of who is a parent

Changes in society have meant that 'given' definitions may no longer be sufficient to operate in practice. With broken and restructured families who counts as a child's 'parent' is no longer a straightforward concept. Schools are required to have a wide range of dealings with a pupil's parents and it is helpful for teachers to know who this might include. Many children are cared for on a daily basis by people who are either carers or extended family members rather than parents. It is important to ensure that the significant people in a child's life, those he or she spends time with and those who have a parental responsibility, are not excluded from decisions. It is worth clarifying at the outset who needs to be invited to meetings, who will be given information and whether there are issues of legal responsibility which the school needs to know about. Sensitivity may be needed here, in particular with some families who have reasons to be anxious about what they may see as interrogation into their private lives. Reasons for ascertaining family information should be made clear. In this text we use the word 'parent' as an inclusive term, encompassing all those who have a parental responsibility towards the child.

## Parents' views

If schools and parents are going to have anything approaching a 'partnership' then the agenda needs to be based on mutual understanding. The main purpose of the research on which the first half of this book is based was to find out from parents and carers themselves what the issues are for them, to explore what may be important in their relationships with schools and which approaches more likely to be met with success. Here we give a voice to that group of parents who have children with special educational needs (SEN) related to emotional, social and behavioural issues. The study that has elicited this information is detailed at the beginning of Chapter 4.

## Teachers' views

Although there are comments from others the predominant views expressed and quoted here are, without apology, those of parents and carers. These include both positive and negative statements about schools, teachers and systems. These are based on parents' own varied experiences, interpreted through their own constructs. Although there are many instances of good practice, and overall a view that home–school relationships are improving, teachers may reasonably feel that this is a one-sided version of what happens in schools and want to defend their position. We hope that readers will view sympathetically the struggle that many parents have to be heard, even though the ways they may do this do not always make it easy to respond positively. In professional development sessions some teachers have argued for sympathy and support when working with parents who do not seem to appreciate or even undermine their efforts on behalf of children. We acknowledge that there are times when teachers meet situations that are exceptionally difficult. Even more frequently, teachers, keen to work constructively with parents, are frustrated that 'it's the ones you need to see most who never come near the school'.

This book is not intended to belittle teachers' professionalism but to explore ways of meeting needs more effectively. The message is that even where parents seem to be intransigently negative there are experiences from their own backgrounds that often explain this. Teachers have choices in the way they approach and respond to parents. Emotionally intelligent interactions that entail 'plugging in' to their concerns and contexts in a real way are worth the effort. As the research illustrates, the better the relationship between home and school, the better the potential outcomes for everyone – the child, the parent and the beleaguered professional in the classroom.

## Outline of content

The following two chapters put the rest of the book into context. They explore the current state of knowledge about the relevant issues. Chapter 2 includes perspectives on behaviour including definition and attribution. Chapter 3 is specifically concerned with parents' roles in school and the issues involved in realising the principle of partnership. Chapter 4 outlines the research study, which explores parents' own views about what they find supportive in school and which factors impede collaboration. Parents' own words are used extensively to illustrate the findings. Chapter 5 looks at the range of outcomes that are linked to different approaches and Chapter 6 outlines a model that schools may use in thinking about how to work most effectively with parents.

It is acknowledged that there may be significant challenges in establishing and maintaining good relationships with some parents and 'working in partnership' is not an easy concept for schools to deliver. The second half of this book addresses the context for specific groups of families. It is hoped that this will give insight into approaches and responses that foster understanding and stimulate creativity in working together.

Chapter 7 is about working with parents who have harmed their children. The emotions for teachers here are some of the most challenging. It is understandable to feel anger and attribute blame when the damage to children is evident. It is also easy to make assumptions and to misjudge not only the facts but also the possibilities. Anna Harskamp has many years' experience of working with families where there are concerns of abuse and the message of her chapter is that one of the best ways of supporting a child's well-being is to find ways of supporting the family. To do this requires both insight and sensitivity.

Chapter 8 is concerned with children who are in 'public care'. These children can be some of the most vulnerable and the most challenging for schools. There are some overlaps here with Chapter 7 and also with Chapter 9 as many of these children are in transient placements. Jean Law looks at the variety of arrangements for the care of children and the implications these have for teachers in working with natural parents, foster carers and residential staff. She also clarifies the importance for children of schooling – the stability it can provide and the opportunities it offers for children whose life expectations may otherwise be less than optimistic.

Chapter 9 raises issues about working with mobile families, whether these families are mobile because of life circumstances, such as asylum seekers or families escaping domestic violence, or a life choice such as Travellers. Anthea Wormington has many years' experience of working in areas in London where mobile families are often a significant proportion of school populations. This throws up many issues that have to be taken into consideration when meeting the needs of pupils and communicating with parents.

Chapter 10 also has some issues in common with Chapter 9 but focuses on the different cultural expectations of families who come from diverse communities. Ann Phoenix looks at what is known from research and provides insight into the different ways children and their families might be construed in education and how school issues may be perceived by different communities.

Chapter 11 introduces solution focused approaches. This structured way of thinking underpins teacher–parent consultations to focus on strengths and possibilities rather than problems. It is a way of putting into operation at an individual level the frameworks described earlier. Elizabeth Gillies writes about her own experiences with this approach to illustrate how it can make a difference to the way parents think about themselves and their abilities to effect positive change for their children.

Finally Chapter 12 reiterates the major messages of the book. It reminds readers that how people think and talk about issues determines what happens in schools. Working with parents presents the best chance of success in both managing and meeting the needs of pupils with behavioural difficulty. This requires a specific approach that is challenging but ultimately optimistic.

## References

Department for Education and Employment (DfEE) (2000) *SEN Code of Practice on the Identification and Assessment of Pupils with Special Educational Needs.* Consultation Document. London: The Stationery Office.

MacLure, M. and Walker, B. (1999) *Secondary School Parents' Evenings.* Report for the Economic and Social Research Council, England and Wales. Norwich: University of East Anglia.

Miller, A. (1994) 'Parents and difficult behaviour: always the problem or part of the solution?', in Gray, P. *et al.* (eds) *Challenging Behaviour in Schools*, 92–107. London: Routledge.

# CHAPTER 2

# Behaviour in School

The research on effective schools mirrors our own experiences . . . the ethos, organisation and working policies in a school make a significant difference to how children's behaviour is perceived and what is put in place to develop appropriate classroom behaviours.          (Roffey and O'Reirdan 2001)

## Introduction

Teachers often have a struggle with pupils who are difficult to manage in the classroom. They have a demanding curriculum to deliver and expectations are on them to ensure that pupils reach attainment targets. Individuals who are disruptive or demand a great deal of attention interfere with that aim. They are not only a problem to themselves but also for the class. Teachers would seem to have less and less time to deal with individuals, at least until that child's needs and demands are so intrusive that something has to be done. At this point teachers are often emotionally involved themselves, with feelings that range from frustration and anger to helplessness and depression. Pupils who are challenging are not only irritating and time consuming but also may invalidate a teacher's professional self-concept by threatening their competence. In the worst scenarios, reactions may become explosive and parents may find themselves at the receiving end of pent-up exasperation. It isn't surprising that 'home–school interviews' can be fraught, and the communication within them less than ideal for a problem-solving framework. This is particularly so when the underlying agenda for a teacher at this stage may be how to have the child removed from their class, if not from the school.

Even where there is a clearly defined and agreed behaviour policy in school the operation of this frequently varies from teacher to teacher depending on their personality, their views of the child and the relationship between them, the teacher's attributions for behaviour and the level of their personal tolerance. There is likely to be as much difference between teachers in one school as there is between schools. This is illustrated by an informal evaluation of a behaviour policy by the author in one secondary school which revealed that several teachers found the system 'too punitive' whereas others were of the opinion that pupils were having an easy ride and 'getting away with things'.

This chapter explores the range of perspectives on what is considered to be 'problem' behaviour and what the research says about different attributions for causality. We then look at behaviour within a SEN framework. We examine the issues for teachers and the fact that management is often their primary concern whereas parents usually want a greater focus on meeting their child's needs. This raises issues of responsibility and who might be expected to do what about behaviour in the school context. Finally we comment on school culture and how this impacts on all of the above. There is a focus throughout on the varying ways parents and teachers construe behavioural issues.

## Perspectives on behaviour

### Definitions of 'problem' behaviour

The extent of difference between parent and teacher definitions of what actually constitutes a problem was one of the major findings of a large study in 1970. This looked at issues for over two thousand children presenting with behavioural difficulties and found that, apart from where there were signs of psychiatric disturbance, there was very little agreement between parents and teachers (Rutter *et al.* 1970). This study has been replicated by subsequent research (McGee *et al.* 1983, in New Zealand; Tizard *et al.* 1988, in England). Within the educational context it is usually the school that maintains control over problem definition. If the student presents difficulties of management for the teacher then their behaviour is seen as the problem. Conversely, teachers are often less prepared to acknowledge difficulties that are brought to their notice by parents (MacLure and Walker 1999). Preparedness to acknowledge the interactive factors within school that may be contributing to the 'problem', such as personality clashes, pedagogic style or inappropriate expectations, seems to be rare. For older students, however, there is an increasing awareness of the need for greater flexibility within the curriculum to address disaffection (DfEE 1999).

## Attribution

How teachers and parents think about behaviour includes what they believe lies behind it – the reasons why a child is well or badly behaved. These attributions make a significant difference to what they think should be done about it and consequently to their interactions with others involved.

Prior to the 1981 Education Act (DES 1981) in England and Wales, the 'within-child' medical model led to pupils being labelled 'maladjusted' and 'treated' for their difficulties. Although factors related to home background were also blamed, it was the child who was often seen as the 'problem'. Intrinsic factors such as personality, attitude, motivation, impulsiveness and 'lack of respect' were all cited as the underlying reasons for bad behaviour. The term 'maladjusted' was in common use and applied to pupils, to the schools they attended and journals specialising in 'problem children'.

Although early school effectiveness literature underlined the fact that schools have an impact on reducing or exacerbating the impact of negative experiences on pupil behaviour (Rutter *et al.* 1979) there is little evidence to suggest that schools find it easy to accept this responsibility. Despite the current perspective on SEN which focuses on systemic and interactive factors to determine need and intervention, 'within-child' models for children with behavioural issues frequently continue to persist (e.g. Upton and Cooper 1990, Miller 1996). Where teachers are more aware of the dangers of labelling they may well look elsewhere than the child for the cause of the behaviour and often point to what might be happening at home. Consequently outside agencies may be seen as the appropriate and often singular response.

Parents of children with disabilities often feel guilty but may receive much sympathy and understanding from others, including teachers. Parents of children with emotional and behavioural needs are, by contrast, often held to be responsible and may be blamed overtly.

Many families have considerable struggles themselves to come to terms with the difficulties their children are presenting. They also look for reasons both within the child and within the school. There is some evidence that parents often feel that if only their children were taught properly all would be well. In one study of a primary school (Cefai 1995) the majority of parents perceived their children's behavioural difficulties as inability to cope with work and/or difficulties with the teacher or authority. Teachers, in the same study, were more concerned about pupils' challenge to their authority or their reluctance to complete schoolwork. They blamed within-child and family factors as the cause of behavioural problems in school. There was little mention of pupils' needs not being met adequately in school.

## Inclusion for special education or exclusion for behaviour?

Some commentators (e.g. Gray 1997) have commented on the worrying and growing separation of emotional and behavioural difficulties (EBD) from consideration of SEN issues in general. Many schools, under increasing pressure to perform well for the benefit of the larger student body, are at a loss to know what to do with and for these disturbed and disturbing youngsters. When there are constant pressures on teachers to be 'effective' in terms of attainment this is likely to have both personal and professional implications. Issues of priorities, time, personal resources and professional reputation may reduce teachers' ability to respond optimally to individuals who are demanding of attention. The same argument could be put forward about interactions with 'difficult' parents.

The inclusion of children with disabilities and other special educational needs within the mainstream has now become an issue of human rights and equality of opportunity. Where special needs include or comprise an emotional/behavioural component, however, there is less support for these views. Children, who arguably should have greatest access to a welcoming and 'normal' environment, are at risk of increasing marginalisation. The 1990s saw a marked increase in the number of pupils who were excluded from school. There were concerns about the young age of some of these children and also about the effects on their future educational attainments. For schools, however, the removal of disruptive individuals is often seen as a solution in that it frees teachers to concentrate on delivering the curriculum – or at least until the next pupil presents similar problems.

Formal exclusions from school in Britain are now more carefully monitored and schools are expected to follow stringent guidelines before a pupil can be officially excluded on a permanent basis. The local authority's behaviour support plan should then identify the alternative educational provision to be made (DfEE 1999). A focus on the problems caused by social exclusion has provided yet another impetus to maintain children within the mainstream wherever possible. The increasing problem of teacher recruitment and retention, however, is to some extent swinging the pendulum back with an emphasis on parental responsibility for behaviour rather than teachers' and a 'softening' of the hard line on exclusions.

Schools are also sensitive to the resource implications of pupils who require additional support, especially if they do not raise the school's reputation for examination success. Despite the rhetoric on the need for inclusion and agreement in principle, where pupils present behavioural difficulties the aim may be to segregate them or at least move them elsewhere. Despite the formal measures to limit exclusions there is evidence that some schools find their own ways to persuade parents to take their child elsewhere.

*'it was never "we are expelling him" but "Before we do, we think it would be better if you found somewhere else."'*                                   *(parent)*

*"'We are sending him home in the afternoons as he can't cope. We are sending him home to avoid excluding him."'*                                   *(SENCO)*

Much of this book stresses the overlap between needs. It is often not a question of learning or behaviour but learning *and* behaviour and usually a high level of emotional needs as well. The re-establishment of behaviour firmly within a special needs framework may well influence the way it is thought about and consequently the actions that are taken about it.

## Needs or management?

There is a dual conceptualisation of difficulties in schools (Miller 1996). Although every child with special educational needs requires a focus on both intervention and management, the management issue for behaviour often becomes paramount for teachers. Finding ways of meeting the needs of both pupils and teachers in the mainstream classroom is of increasing concern. We know there are some things that work better than others, but there is also evidence that schools are often unwilling or unable to put these into place in a consistent way (Miller 1996).

One of the main blocks to successful home–school collaboration is the potential difference in the agenda that exists at a joint meeting. Parents may arrive with overriding concerns about their child and the situation he or she and they find themselves in. This may range from anxiety about their child's happiness, or progress, to embarrassment that they are being 'shown up'. Their first concern is not about how the behaviour can be managed at school, or access to the curriculum for the other pupils. Although there may be a genuine concern for the needs of the pupil, management of the 'problem' is, however, often a major focus for teachers. Consequently they want parents to 'do' something that will ease the difficulties they are experiencing in doing their job properly. Often there is little clarity about what that 'something' is and parents may leave such meetings feeling confused, de-skilled and blamed.

Macbeth (1984) reported on school–family relations in the countries of the European Community and found that parents and teachers were frequently involved in blaming and not communicating with each other. The child was therefore engaged in different sets of relations with opportunities for playing one off against the other.

## Responsibility for action

There is agreement within many studies about the lack of school action resulting from parent–teacher consultations. As we have seen, parents often consider that the child's problem in school is the school's responsibility but schools frequently think otherwise. Parents are often expected to take action over problems raised by teachers but may have difficulty securing undertakings from teachers to act. Lack of action by schools is an issue for parents who may feel that nothing is done in school prior to the involvement of an external agent.

Dowling (1990) describes three possible different scenarios for action that are commonplace in school:

- the family attributes the child's problems to issues in school and expects the school to deal with it
- the school considers that it does all it can but given the family circumstances does not expect any change
- the family and school agree that the child needs help and sets about looking for an 'expert' who will provide it.

Cefai's (1995) study describes initial school actions taken by teachers that are overwhelmingly focused on punishment and sanctions. Parents were often involved when these early strategies did not work, rather than when the concern was first raised. A few teachers and parents found that informal and positive home–school interaction had beneficial outcomes but over half the parents voiced complaints about the procedures that were put in place to involve them, describing them as 'inappropriate', 'embarrassing' and 'disconcerting'. Although the majority of parents and teachers expressed a desire for closer home–school cooperation there was no agreement about how that should take place or that it should be on an equal basis.

## The power of school culture

The second story at the beginning of the first chapter illustrates the power of school culture. Dee felt safe in expressing her frustrations in the staff room, needed support from a colleague and got it. All of which may be viewed positively. But her perceptions and proposed solutions remained unchallenged. Alice agreed with everything Dee said and reinforced the prevailing view of the child and the family. It might have made Dee feel better in herself but the outcome was also a feeling of helplessness to effect change.

School culture dictates not only what happens but also how things are done. It influences expectations for behaviour 'how we do things around here', not only for pupils but also for staff. According to Miller (1996) even with friendly colleagues many teachers feel alone when dealing with behavioural issues in the classroom. Good home–school partnerships where there is a 'shared endeavour' have the potential to alleviate this sense of isolation.

## Summary

School effectiveness studies have underlined the fact that what goes on in schools makes a difference to the incidence of poor behaviour. Even within areas with a similar intake some schools are successful in reducing incidents of unacceptable behaviour and others seem to exacerbate difficulties for children, who then become even more badly behaved. School culture is communicated both to the people who work and study within the organisation and to the parents about their place. How parents respond to that culture either reinforces it or challenges it. Most parents do not have the inside knowledge, skills or confidence to do other than accept the role that is offered to them. Some do so from awareness of their child's vulnerability in the school system. Those who do not, either by an aggressive stance or by withdrawing from contact, are usually considered part of the problem, which has implications for partnership. This is the focus on the next chapter.

## References

Ball, M. (1998) *Disabled Children: Directions for their future care.* Wetherby, Yorkshire: Social Care Group, Department of Health and the Council for Disabled Children.

Campion, J. (1984) 'Psychological services for children: using family therapy in the setting of a school psychological service', *Journal of Family Therapy* **6**, 47–62.

Cefai, C. (1995) 'Investigation of pupils', parents' and teachers' perceptions of behaviour problems and school–family interactions in a mainstream primary school'. MSc. thesis, University of Wales, Swansea.

Connor, M. J. (1998) *Parent/Carer Views on Support for Children with Emotional and Behavioural Difficulties.* Guildford: Surrey County Council Educational Psychology Service.

Croll, P. and Moses, D. (1985) *Preventing Classroom Disruption, Policy, Practice and Evaluation in Urban Schools.* London: Croom Helm.

Department for Education and Employment (DfEE) (1999) *Social Inclusion: Pupil support.* Circular 10/99. London: The Stationery Office.

Department of Education and Science (DES) (1981) Education Act. London: HMSO.

Dowling, E. (1990) 'Children's disturbing behaviour: whose problem is it? An account of a school based service for parents and teachers', *Association of Child Psychology and Psychiatry Newsletter* **12**(4), 8–11.

Gray, P. (1997) 'Policy in a world of emotions: where to now with EBD?', in Norwich, B. (ed.) *Inclusion or Exclusion: Future policy for emotional and behavioural difficulties. Special Educational Needs Policy Options Steering Group*, 22–37. Tamworth: NASEN.

Macbeth, A. (1984) 'The child between: a report on school–family relations in countries of the European Community', EEC studies collection, *Education Series* **13**.

MacLure, M. and Walker, B. (1999) *Secondary School Parents' Evenings*. Report for the Economic and Social Research Council, England and Wales. Norwich: University of East Anglia.

McGee, R. *et al.* (1983) 'Parents and teachers' perceptions of behaviour problems in seven year old children', *The Exceptional Child* **30**(2), 151–61.

Miller, A. (1996) *Pupil Behaviour and Teacher Culture*. London: Cassell.

Roffey, S. and O'Reirdan, T. (2001) *Young Children and Classroom Behaviour*. London: David Fulton Publishers.

Rutter, M. *et al.* (1970) *Education, Health and Behaviour*. London: Longman.

Rutter. M. *et al.* (1979) *Fifteen Thousand Hours*. London: Open Books.

Tizard, B. *et al.* (1988) *Young Children at School in the Inner City*. Hove, Sussex: Laurence Erlbaum Associates.

Upton, G. and Cooper, P. (1990) 'A new perspective on behaviour problems in schools: the eco-systemic approach', *Maladjustment and Therapeutic Education* **8**(1), 3–18.

# CHAPTER 3

# School and Family Partnership

Children's progress will be limited if their parents are not seen as partners in the educational process with unique knowledge, and information to impart.

(DfE 1994)

## Introduction

This chapter begins by setting out the way parents have been viewed in education in the past and the situation now. These are both expectations as determined by law and guidance and the reality as perceived by parents. We look at differences in the ways schools may respond to parents of children with special educational needs, depending on the difficulties their child is presenting. We summarise research where parents have said what they value and need and the issues that have affected their partnership with schools. The focus is specifically on what is happening at the home–school interface, rather than partnership between parents and the local authority or agencies. All quotes without a reference are from parents in the study detailed in the next chapter.

Partnership is a slippery concept. The word is bandied about freely in all sorts of contexts but the perception of what constitutes 'partnership' differs widely. Even the legislation and guidance does not provide much clarification. At the very least partnership assumes participation in joint ventures but it also has connotations that suggest equality. Entirely equitable distribution of responsibility is probably unrealistic but fundamentally home–school partnership must be a shared endeavour.

'The school has been working in partnership with us since the new head arrived . . . its both sides recognising that they have a common problem, a common interest and wish to assist each other in providing a commonly agreed result.'

Some education professionals are reluctant to use the term 'partnership' when it comes to talking about home–school relations. Their view is that power ultimately remains with the school and it is within the school's gift to facilitate liaison and empower parents, not the other way round. For some, partnership is more a process of development than a static state.

> Partnership has different connotations to different people, according to their role, status, functions. The view that it is less an end state than it is a dynamic, evolving process is borne out by the research. Progression towards partnership requires continuing vigilance by the practitioners and parents alike to achieve. Its expression comes in parents manifestly being consulted and supported on a basis of equality, openness and mutual respect . . . to be central in decision making on behalf of their children.                                    (Wolfendale and Cook 1997)

There is a risk, however, in assuming agreement between partners about the agenda towards which they are working. The issue here is how to achieve that mutuality in the first place so that both teachers and parents see partnership as a real possibility, want it and see themselves as active and effective within it.

## An overview of the place of parents/carers in education

The place of parents and parental rights in education has been a major theme of the last two decades. How families have been conceptualised within the school context has, however, developed considerably over time.

### *Parents as a resource for learning*

It is widely accepted that regular home–school contact and parental encouragement enhances children's progress. This co-educator view has been confirmed over the years by a number of projects, such as home–school reading schemes. These relationships have, however, usually been organised on 'professional' terms with little acknowledgement of parental skill or a genuine attempt to empower parents within a partnership approach. Many schools today look to parents themselves as a resource, for example help with reading and maths, or on the resources at home, for example computer facilities to research information for assignments. There is obvious inequality between families when it comes to material goods; the inequality is less clear with respect to less tangible resources at home such as time, space and skills.

## Parents as a support for the school

Parent support includes the inevitable fund-raising, help in the classroom and at times as a pressure group. These aspects of parental involvement continue to be common everywhere but often exclude sections of the parent community for both practical and social/cultural reasons. It is, for instance, difficult for parents who work full time, have care commitments or lack English language skills to become part of the school support network. It also takes a high level of confidence to approach an existing group even if the people within it are open and accepting.

## Parents as consumers of education services

Schools have come under increasing pressure to alter their view of parents from being passive recipients of their services to being accountable to them. In England and Wales, *The Parents' Charter* (DES 1991) was intended to give parents rights to express a preference for a school, to knowing how well their children are doing and how well their child's school is doing in relation to other schools. Parents have representation on governing bodies and have to be consulted during school inspections. These parental rights are at times exercised in relation to the rights of 'other children' to be 'protected' from individuals with difficulties. It is not unknown for parents to lobby for the exclusion of certain pupils. This potentially puts well-meaning schools in a dilemma about collective responsibility for all children.

## Parents as partners

This theme is now rooted in educational discourse in general but is particularly high on the agenda in relation to individual children with special educational needs. Teachers generally want parents to be involved. Parents, despite their anxieties and practical issues, usually want to try to support their children. In many cases the motivation to collaborate is there and at least on the surface there is already a shared agenda.

## Rhetoric and reality

There has been a great deal of nodding in the direction of 'partnership' and in some ways parents have more say in education now than ever before. The rhetoric that abounds within law and guidance, however, is not necessarily transformed into practice.

## Awareness

Most teachers accept that greater parental interest and support leads to improved pupil achievement. In many schools parents are welcomed and involved in a wide variety of roles. There is also an indication that parents are more aware of their rights but putting these into practice is a different matter.

> Many parents are now beginning to sense their entitlement to information, to have a say and to be listened to, even if in reality, many find it difficult to achieve this, and many schools do not encourage it . . . In spite of its tangible benefits and positive achievements, home–school work in Britain continues to be surrounded by deep, intractable and problematic issues.
> (Wolfendale 1992: 2)

One of these issues has been identified as the need for sensitivity, special skills and experience at the home–school interface.

## Relationships in schools

New perspectives on the roles and rights of parents have occurred at the same time as many other initiatives and innovations within education. This has put unprecedented pressure on teachers. It would be unsurprising if work with parents is sometimes viewed as a mixed blessing and teachers perceive formal links with parents as yet another competing demand on their time and limited resources. It follows that individual parents who are 'uncooperative' or 'demanding' may be seen as a hindrance rather than as partners in the process of education. Teachers and parents would seem to have expectations of each other that do not always foster collaboration (Hanko 1999).

Professional dominance is still much in evidence. Vincent's research (1996) found that 40 per cent of the 95 parents she interviewed found visiting schools intimidating, several mentioned that teachers 'talked down' to them and others related incidents in which they felt they had been put firmly in their place. Although particular teachers were praised for their friendliness, parents did not necessarily receive more detailed or exact information about their child. Parents did not know what questions to ask and occasionally teachers assumed knowledge that parents did not have.

Many parents find the physical environment of a secondary school intimidating, carrying memories of powerlessness and failure from their own school days.

Schools can appear full of adults, with their expertise and incomprehensible jargon, apparently waiting to make judgements of their child and implicitly on their parenting . . . There is a need to think very carefully about the welcome and care parents receive when they do come into school.                                        (Beresford and Hardie 1996: 140)

These authors also make the point that schools need to ensure that they provide opportunities to communicate positive achievements to parents. They comment that one secondary school on reviewing letters home discovered that 95 per cent of them were negative. Beresford and Hardie conclude that a wide range of skills is required for developing home–school relations. These are very different from the skills of managing children in a classroom situation and teachers often do not recognise the skills that are needed.

## Pressure on school places

The reality in many areas is that school places are limited, leading to little more than an illusion of free choice within the state system. The consequences of the market model have serious implications for perpetuating inequality. Parents who can afford it move into the 'right' catchment areas for the 'good schools' and the rights of parents of pupils who may have a high level of need but do not enhance the reputation of the school may become very thin on the ground.

## Parents' perceptions of home–school relationships

The views of teachers about the effectiveness of home–school links do not always tally with those of parents. Although parents have a strong desire to know more about what is going on in school, existing channels of communication are not often seen as an effective way of consulting or disseminating information. Although parents are involved in many ways at school it is the establishment of effective two-way communication channels which seems to be the prerequisite to many other activities.

A study by the National Foundation for Educational Research (NFER) (Jowett *et al.* 1991) showed that there were examples of good practice but also many concerns about process and how interactions took place within schools. Many of the findings have been replicated by other more recent research and by the present study.

The NFER research found that it was not unusual for parents to say that they did not understand what went on in schools and how different it all seemed from their own school days.

*'I think there should be a phase of induction for parents when their children first go to school; someone needs to sit down and explain to them exactly what happens . . .'*

School policies and practices were usually presented as unalterable facts without explanation or discussion. Parents did not necessarily understand the reasons why things were done as they were or the thinking behind policies. This often left parents worried that they had been trying to do the best for their children but approaching it 'all wrong'; they felt de-skilled and guilty. There was limited routine contact with staff and for most parents this was considered to be rather superficial. Contact was 'problem focused' and there was little evidence of ongoing contact about children's learning and development.

*'At one parents' evening my son's teacher said that he had nothing to say to me as there were no problems.'*

There was a lack of clarity about the purpose of meetings or the desired outcome of home–school contact.

*'They expected me to work miracles and I couldn't do it.'*

Although the NFER research found that there was a general belief in the responsiveness of staff, it was clear that there was potential for significant conflict when disagreements or breakdowns in communication occurred. There were situations where parents had been dissatisfied with how their concerns had been dealt with when complex issues were being discussed. In general parents felt that teachers tended to defend their position rather than share their concerns. Parents had often heard only negative comments about their children. One mother told a member of a Parental Involvement in Education Team that she was

*'the only person who ever says anything nice about my child'.*

The NFER research overall found that existing structures for involvement readily produced a division between parents who came into school and who were perceived to be interested in, or indeed care about, their children and those who were not. Teachers often failed to appreciate the practical problems faced by parents who could not fully participate in planned activities.

*'If my boss knew how much time I'd spent running backwards and forwards to hospitals, nursery . . . I'd never have kept my job, never.'*

Hanko's experience in schools also suggests that teachers have more success in establishing positive relationships when they look beyond the immediate to discover what might underlie parental hostility. 'Whether teachers manage to initiate a supportive relationship or unwittingly collude with parents' negative expectations, will at least in part depend on their own understanding of such issues and their reactions to parents behaviour' (Hanko 1999).

As well as identifying the need to convey information in a way that is accessible to all parents there was also the question of ethos and coherent whole-school policies about relationships with parents.

> A pleasant and welcoming approach to parents is vital. The mother who was not allowed to hand over cash in school for her child's lunch because it was not in an envelope and who was made to feel like a naughty child; the parents who arrived in a secondary school one dark winter's evening and spent more than ten minutes searching for the non-signposted staff room and the mother who left open evenings feeling that she was being judged as a parent are all absorbing messages about the institution called 'school' that will adversely influence their response to invitations to participate further.                    (Jowett *et al.* 1991: 141)

Atkin and Bastiani's research (1984) had concluded that much remained to be done in both initial training and in-service training. This was confirmed in the NFER study where only three teachers had had any initial training in working with parents. It was recommended that staff needed well-developed communication skills, especially if they were to enter into the more ambitious dialogue with parents that was attempted in some schools. 'There is a need for in-service training in the practicalities of working with parents; some of it at the level of social skills . . . it is crucial that staff are aware of the impact that their statements can have' (Atkin and Bastiani 1984: 144).

## Partnership with parents of children with special educational needs

The concept of 'partnership' now has prominence within the SEN legislation. The term implies a certain kind of relationship which in reality is hard to establish and maintain. It implies mutual understanding and respect, shared aims and objectives, a consensual approach and a level of equality of power as well as knowledge and skill. Vincent (1996) expresses concern about the terminology that has been used in relation to parents' relationship with education professionals, considering that it is simplistic, imprecise and open to misappropriation. The word 'empowerment' is also potentially misleading and inaccurate. Wolfendale (1992) finds 'enabling' more useful as a description. With differences in perception, expectations and priorities it is unsurprising that anxiety about blame may arise on both sides and trust difficult to establish.

## The views of parents of children with SEN on 'partnership'

At a centre for families with children who had just been diagnosed with SEN mothers were asked what they most appreciated (Dale 1996). Forty per cent of them cited emotional support, care and concern for themselves as well as their child and the same percentage remarked upon the practical guidance and concrete advice. Dale cites research that shows that interventions emphasising the importance of the parent–child relationship and offering parents relationship-focused support have beneficial effects on parental confidence (Affleck *et al.* 1982). Beveridge (1997), reporting on interviews with parents of children with SEN, confirms that it is the quality of the interaction in schools and the process of communication that is important. Although schools believe that working with parents is beneficial and think that they are doing this, parents' views do not always match those of teachers. Partnership is not only about listening to parents but also valuing their contribution and keeping them properly informed about what is happening for their child. Even where behaviour is not an issue parents feel that teachers attribute difficulties, at least in part, to assumptions about the child and home circumstances. Beveridge concludes that, among other things, teachers need to recognise the personal and emotional investment of parents, recognise children's strengths as well as weaknesses, support parents in the preparation of their contributions, respect the validity of differing perspectives and seek ways of reconciling different views. Mallett (1997), writing as a parent, confirms many of the same issues and talks about partnership being more than just a good relationship; 'actions' in school need to follow on from good interactions in meetings. It can be especially hard for parents to express their frustration if it puts at risk seemingly positive relationships.

*'If it takes six months (to get help) and we just talk about it a lot then it's just a waste of time.'*

Wolfendale and Cook (1997) evaluated 26 parent partnership schemes throughout the UK. The parent groups had divergent views about parent partnership schemes in connection with home–school relationships. Some felt that having a parent supporter meant that schools listened more, while others commented that schools were hostile. Forty-three per cent of respondents, however, were in support of schools and teachers. Twenty-six per cent of parents felt that schools had learnt from parents since the start of the scheme: 'Schools are beginning to set the ground rules for communication, the way one is spoken to is different . . . however the outcomes remain the same' (Wolfendale and Cook 1997: 99). There were few instances, however, of respondents being unequivocal that partnership goals had been achieved, particularly so at the home–school interface. Practice was considered to be inconsistent. Specific concerns were related to the need to reach parents from ethnic minorities and to the support that is needed in schools to evolve a range of strategies to draw parents in.

## 'Partnership' with parents of children with emotional and behavioural difficulties

Gray (1997) writes about how children with EBD are marginalised within the SEN framework and the same appears to be true of their parents. Although teachers often say that the support of parents in meeting the needs of children with behavioural difficulties is crucial, communication between home and school with regard to behavioural difficulties is often limited. It is also more likely to happen when things have reached a crisis and then not in a collaborative framework. Whereas special educational needs are usually seen as the outcome of misfortune, behavioural difficulties are construed as someone's fault. This is often considered to be parental neglect or mismanagement.

*'They spoke down to me as to make me feel I'd been a bad parent.'*

Although behavioural difficulties in school are frequently attributed to parenting styles and other family factors, Miller found evidence that resolution is often attributed to school intervention and not to changes at home (Miller 1996).

Wolfendale (1993) found that parents' views were not routinely incorporated into school actions and that a number of practical difficulties prevented a positive home–school partnership from developing. She listed the following as widening the perception gap:

- While schools often used letters of complaint, positive letters were rarely sent home.
- Many schools tended to underestimate or even ignore school-based factors involved in behaviour problems.
- Some schools involved parents only as a last resort.
- Schools were not always welcoming places for parents.
- Liaison with parents took time, which teachers may have difficulty in finding.

- Many teachers felt that parents were to blame for much misbehaviour in schools.
- Some parents were not willing to cooperate with schools and teachers in dealing with and preventing behavioural problems.

The fact that learning needs and behavioural needs are often simultaneously present in the same child is not always acknowledged (Ball 1998).

## Elusive parents

Teachers, ready and willing to be 'partners', are often exasperated by parents who are rarely seen in school. Bridges (1987) investigated the views of parents who rarely came to school and found that instead of apathy about their children, there was a range of practical and confidence issues that made it more difficult for them to attend. The most recurring theme was the dread that parents felt about entering school, mostly related to their own childhood experiences. If this was how parents felt before there was any mention of concern about their children's behaviour, it is not difficult to imagine the range of emotions and reactions that might ensue when a request was made to attend to discuss a potentially contentious issue. Parents have many reasons for staying away and schools need to take these into account when making initial overtures.

*'I hated school. I was called names and I was always scared they would ask me to read.'*

## Summary

There are many examples of casework where the development of a positive home–school relationship has had considerable benefits to all concerned, including an improvement in behaviour (Gupta *et al.* 1990, Topping 1992). Pupils themselves are responsive to parents being sent positive messages from school both in the secondary (Caffyn 1989) and in the primary sectors (Harrop and Williams 1992).

The interface between home and school, however, continues to be problematic at all levels. Partnership in general is developing slowly but despite legislation to increase the say that parents have in the education of their children, the power base remains within schools and parents do not always feel comfortable in that environment. Although their contribution to children's education is well recognised there are mixed feelings by teachers towards increased parental involvement.

The picture is more positive in respect of parents of children with SEN, especially where those needs have been identified and outside agencies have become involved. There are continuing problematic issues about relationships and actions at the early stage of identification when schools are dealing with the child's needs themselves.

Home–school collaboration for children with EBD is beset by differences in priorities, perceptions, definitions and structural issues. A number of authors have raised their concerns about communication between schools and families and the incorporation of the parental perspective, especially when problems arise.

It would be a mistake not to acknowledge that some families who have children with behavioural difficulty can be the most challenging to work with and make the most demands on teacher professionalism. Teachers will have come across parents they have considered to be unreasonable, absent, aggressive, over-protective, uncaring, abusive, demanding or irresponsible. They may be seen as undermining the teachers' efforts or the cause of their child's distress. There are often strong emotions involved in working with these parents, from anger and contempt to frustration and despair. Teachers need to acknowledge their own feelings and think about how to structure support for themselves – but also hold on to their own professional integrity by continuing to look for ways of fostering active and positive partnership.

Teachers generally want parents to be involved. Parents, despite their fears and practical issues, usually want to try to support their children. What needs to happen in school to facilitate a mutually supportive partnership when difficulties arise? Good practice does take place. What do parents see as good practice and what discourages them from constructive dialogue with schools? There are many indications that individual teachers are developing their own practices in facilitating partnership with parents. Schools need to support and extend the good practice that already exists; it is within their power to do so. We hope that the following chapters will give insight into how to do this more effectively.

## References

Affleck, G. *et al.* (1982) 'Promise of relationship-focused early intervention in developmental disabilities', *Journal of Special Education* **16**, 413–30.

Atkin, J. and Bastiani, J. (1984) *Preparing Teachers to Work with Parents: A survey of initial training*. Nottingham: University of Nottingham School of Education.

Ball, M. (1998) *Disabled Children: Directions for their future care*. Wetherby, Yorkshire: Social Care Group, Department of Health and the Council for Disabled Children.

Beresford, E. and Hardie, A. (1996) 'Parents and secondary schools: a different approach?', in Bastiani, J. and Wolfendale, S. (eds) *Home–School Work in Britain*. London: David Fulton Publishers.

Beveridge, S. (1997) 'Implementing partnership with parents in schools', in Wolfendale, S. (ed.) *Working with Parents of SEN Children After the Code of Practice*. London: David Fulton Publishers.

Bridges, D. (1987) 'It's the ones who never turn up that you really want to see: the problem of the non-attending parent', in Bastiani, J. (ed.) *Parents and Teachers*. Slough: NFER.

Caffyn, R. E. (1989) 'Attitudes of British secondary school teachers and pupils to rewards and punishments', *Educational Research* **31**(3), 210–20.

Dale, N. (1996) *Working with Families of Children with Special Educational Needs: Partnership and practice*. London: Routledge.

Department for Education (DfE) (1994) *Code of Practice on the Identification and Assessment of Special Educational Needs*. London: The Stationery Office.

Department of Education and Science (DES) (1991) *The Parents' Charter: You and your child's education*. London: HMSO.

Gray, P. (1997) 'Policy in a world of emotions: where to now with EBD?', in Norwich, B. (ed.) *Inclusion or Exclusion: Future policy for emotional and behavioural difficulties. Special Educational Needs Policy Options Steering Group*, 22–37. Tamworth: NASEN.

Gupta, R. *et al.* (1990) 'A study of the effectiveness of home-based reinforcement in a secondary school', *Educational Psychology in Practice* **5**(4), 197–200.

Hanko, G. (1999) *Increasing Competence through Collaborative Problem-Solving*. London: David Fulton Publishers.

Harrop, A. and Williams, T. (1992) 'Rewards and punishments in the primary school: pupils' perceptions and teachers' usage', *Educational Psychology in Practice* **7**(4), 211–15.

Jowett, S. *et al.* (1991) *Building Bridges: Parental involvement in schools*. Windsor: NFER Nelson.

Mallett, R. (1997) 'A parental perspective on partnership', in Wolfendale, S. (ed.) *Working with Parents of SEN Children After the Code of Practice*. London: David Fulton Publishers.

Miller, A. (1996) *Pupil Behaviour and Teacher Culture*. London: Cassell.

Tizard, B. *et al.* (1981) *Involving Parents in Nursery and Infant School*. London: Grant McIntyre.

Topping, K. J. (1992) 'School-based behaviour management work with families', *Pastoral Care in Education* **10**(1), 7–17.

Vincent, C. (1996) *Parents and Teachers: Power and participation*. London: Falmer Press.

Wolfendale, S. (1992) *Empowering Parents and Teachers: Working for children*. London: Cassell.

Wolfendale, S. (1993) 'Parents and teachers working together on the assessment of children's progress', in Leadbetter, P. and Leadbetter, J. (eds) *Special Children: Meeting the challenge in the primary school*. London: Cassell.

Wolfendale, S. and Cook, G. (1997) *Evaluation of Parent Partnership Schemes*. DfEE Research Report Number 34. London: The Stationery Office.

CHAPTER 4

# The Voice of Parents

## Introduction

It's hard enough being a parent. Families with children who experience
difficulty with their education often have an even tougher time. They have
to organise themselves, their work and family commitments to attend
meetings, learn the jargon, understand the legalities, help with extra activities and be seen to support their child while meeting the needs of everyone else. Having children with special educational needs potentially puts
considerable strain on individuals and on relationships within the family.

Parents of children with learning, physical or sensory needs usually have
one or more support networks available to them. There are organisations
within which parents of children with SEN can make their voices heard. This
is not so true for those families with children whose SEN are predominantly
behavioural. Many families in the study described below spoke about their
feelings of loneliness and isolation, their sense of guilt and inadequacy and
frequently their perception of being blamed. Most were also anxious about
what was happening or not happening for their child. Sometimes parents
had to shout to be heard and others simply stopped trying.

This chapter is intended to give a voice to this largely unheard group of
parents/carers. Quotes are taken verbatim from interviews to illustrate
parents' concerns and what makes a difference for them in their interactions with schools.

## The research study

The study on which this and the following two chapters are based was less
concerned with measurement than with meaning. The aim was to discover
what families find more supportive or less supportive in their interactions
with schools over issues concerning their child's behaviour. What do the

different experiences parents have in schools mean for them? What helps them feel good about their interactions with teachers and what is off-putting, unhelpful or distressing?

The study investigated the perceptions, beliefs, attitudes, understanding and feelings of parents related to their experiences in schools. It explored the constructs that underpinned their expectations, approaches and responses to events. People are neither culture-free nor value-free. They are bound up with experiences that affect the way they think and feel about things. These are:

- personal, which influence the ways in which they have learnt to make sense of the world
- the constructs of the culture and society in which they live and which also shape their views and responses.

Both of these are, of course, interdependent. Although constructs are not fixed, people do tend to try to place new experiences within a context that has meaning for them and individual constructs are a powerful filter for the interpretation of events. Therefore we were looking both at what parents/carers found supportive or not in school and also at what they themselves brought to that situation.

## Strategies and process

Over 115 individuals took part in the study, which was based in grounded theory. The three interconnected parts of the data collection (focus groups, questionnaire and interviews) built on each other. There were two focus groups of individuals who worked in schools as either teachers or external agencies. The second group comprised English speaking members of local communities. Much of their support work in schools was related to behaviour and they were able to give insight into the views and concerns of non-English speaking families. Questionnaires were sent to all families in one education authority where an educational psychologist had been consulted about their child's behaviour. Seventy-seven were returned with a number of respondents indicating their willingness to be interviewed. Nineteen semi-structured interviews were then carried out, sometimes with more than one family member. Although all participants now lived in one London borough, many had also lived elsewhere and spoke of experiences in other parts of the city and the country. In order to make the interview sample more representative and not unduly weighted to white families with boys, not all volunteers were included and other families were asked to contribute.

## Findings

Qualitative research does not assume that the world is predictable or that there is a linear cause and effect when so many interactive, intrapersonal, interpersonal and socio/cultural variables contribute to a phenomenon. Everyone is different and the participants in this study were no exception. They had varied experiences of schools, teachers and children's behaviour, a range of different emphases and concerns and different ways of handling situations. Although the study has limitations in the self-selected, predominantly female, English speaking sample, what is important are the strong threads that emerged. These describe and illuminate the home–school interface from the perspectives of this group of parents and consequently offer suggestions about the frameworks that might be developed to facilitate partnership. It is these findings that are the focus of the following chapters. Many of these reflect and extend what is known from earlier research.

## Facts and figures

Although many findings from the questionnaire were explored in more depth in the interviews it is worth noting a few points that arose from this part of the study.

- 83.1% of the children in question were male.
- 46% had concerns about behaviour first raised by others at age 4 or below. There is a second surge of concern at 11 years – the age of secondary transfer.
- In over 50% of cases the child with the difficulty was the eldest in the family or the only child.
- 23% of respondents had early concerns about the child's learning and 63% of respondents said their child now had learning difficulties.
- Although 27.3% of parents mentioned direct loss issues for children at home, only 15% acknowledged the impact of rejection and loss on their child and/or attributed their child's difficulties to this.

## Boys and behaviour

It is widely accepted that boys have more identified special needs than girls. The imbalance in the ratio increases significantly both with communication difficulties and with behavioural difficulties. This finding is therefore no surprise. It was not, however, a focus for this particular study and not explored further here.

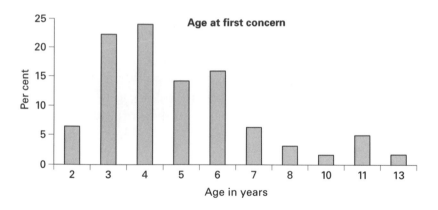

**Figure 4.1** Age at first concern

## Age at first concern

The very young age at which behavioural difficulties are often first identified (see Figure 4.1) may be linked to other issues expanded on in the
interviews. Several parents said that they had no benchmark on which to
make judgements about their children's behaviour. This was especially true
for first time parents. They didn't know what was 'normal' and some pointed
out that they did not know how to manage difficulties when they arose.

*'I feel I'm fumbling around in the dark – what am I going to compare him
with? I haven't got any other kids – I've no female friends with kids. I've not
a clue what I'm supposed to do, unless I look it up in a book.'*
*(Single parent of boy aged 4)*

Alternatively they dealt with behaviour in the same way that their parents
had done.

*'(My daughter's) first teacher offered me some support and I found I was
able to talk to her. She was a West Indian teacher and she says: "You can't
discipline (your daughter) the way you were disciplined. That was cruel."
She was able to say things to me on a level that would really hit home and
ring bells. She understood where I was coming from.'*
*(This parent was also Black British of African-Caribbean descent)*

Other parents also looked to teachers for guidance.

*'Because we never had children before I looked to the teachers who have
the experience . . . we looked to them for advice.'*

An issue for some families was the difficulty of gaining good quality early
assessment.

*'We feel angry that (our son's) requirements were not diagnosed correctly and early enough.'*

## Learning and behaviour difficulties

There is now much evidence to link behaviour and learning difficulties. A child may exhibit one or more of the following:

- immature behaviour that is typical of a more slowly developing child
- specific learning difficulties
- the struggle to learn which stems from emotional issues which may also affect behaviour.

This has implications both at home and at school. Expectations that children cannot meet may lead to behaviour that is difficult to manage. Many parents spoke about the judgements and assumptions that were made about their children and about themselves which were at best inappropriate and at worst exacerbated the difficulties and threatened collaboration. More than anything this highlights the need for an 'open mind' and not jumping to conclusions about what is happening.

*'In the beginning they were quite happy to assume there must be a problem at home.'*

*'I knew he had some sort of problem and I wanted help from the school to find out what this problem was and I think they just thought that he was just a naughty, disruptive child who really didn't want to come to school.'*
*(Parent talking about infant aged child)*

Many parents felt that their anxiety about their children's learning was not mirrored in schools where the focus was on behaviour.

## Behaviour and loss

Many young people are struggling with anger and distress linked to a major loss in their lives, often as a result of family breakdown. As evidenced by this study, the impact for children is not always acknowledged. Even where it is, families are not always prepared to tell the school.

*'His father and I split up in March and he seemed OK. But now A. has started wetting the bed and I know he's eating secretly and that's a comfort thing . . . but I don't want to go into my private details with the school.'*
*(Parent of child aged 12)*

Even where there is an attempt to let schools know circumstances for children teachers do not necessarily know how best to address these issues.

*'I did explain to them how S. had stopped seeing his mum and how this had a big impact on him – but they weren't very supportive at all and said he should be moved to a school for children with behavioural problems.'*

*(Carer of child aged 5)*

## Parent attributions for behaviour

Many parents did not give any reason for their child's difficulties and simply described what their child did or did not do without any attempt at explanation. Many seemed bewildered by how their child was behaving. One parent said she was *'at a complete loss to understand'* and another *'it must be me'*. Although many parents cited school factors, most of these were not seen as the impetus for the initial difficulty but as compounding and exacerbating what was happening for the child. This could be either relationships within school and/or access to the curriculum.

*'He has a learning problem but no one would do anything about it. He ended up being disruptive because he couldn't do his work and it just got worse and worse from then on really.'*

## What do parents/carers find more supportive or less supportive in their interactions with schools?

Parents had varied experiences in different schools and with different teachers. It was rare for anyone to be either entirely negative or entirely positive about what had happened for them and for their child. Overall the impression was that things were often better in the junior school though there was a wide divergence among different institutions across the phases of education. This parent had had a particularly positive experience in her child's primary school and was now struggling with the differences at secondary level.

*'In the primary school you are given a chance to air your opinion, they ask you what you think, do you agree with this or not. But in secondary school everything is set already. In the primary school it is the child who comes first, but here the (secondary) school have their own procedures and rules and things.'*

Nevertheless, it was the individual attitudes, skills and responses of class teachers that appeared to have greatest influence on interactions and outcomes. Teachers who were accepting of the child, able to see both strengths as well as weaknesses and who genuinely valued the parents' input stood out for these families as shining lights in what was often a bleak educational landscape.

*'I had a lot of dealing at that time with (a particular teacher) and the relationship, I couldn't fault it – it was superb, very supportive ongoing communication – a feeling we were doing it together.'*

This same family had not always had such a good experience.

*'The worst was being ostracised and completely unsupported – the school really disowning the situation.'*

The leadership of the head teacher and ethos of the school make a significant difference to how pupils and their parents are perceived and the expectations placed upon staff.

*'They've got a new head in who's the business; I've every faith in her.'*

*'We were afraid to raise issues in the school because the head was very dominating and we were afraid that this would impact on our child.'*

## Communications

Parents want to know what is going on for their child in school. They prefer informal contact that is positive, regular, private, planned, non-intrusive, two-way and early enough to make a difference.

*'If he wanted to talk to you he'd say: "Can I have a word", you know, privately. He was really good at that, I liked him.'*

*'If you're going to have these meetings they need to happen frequently enough to make a difference.'*

*'I can phone the school and leave a message (about things that have happened at home) and they understand. That's been helpful to act as a brake so the difficulties don't just escalate and escalate.'*

Parents are prepared to hear about difficulties and be 'realistic' so long as that is within a framework of acceptance of the whole child.

*'The discussion went well because the teacher said we had a few children like that and they settle down.'*

Communications that focus predominantly or even exclusively on the negative, label the child and/or demand unspecified parent action are not welcome and for many parents raise considerable anxiety or engender anger.

*'I used to be called into meetings and it was all very negative: "your son's this and this and this". I don't remember anyone saying anything positive . . . I was losing all my fight because it was just getting so bad.'*

Communications that do not take account of the context for the parent also have far-reaching consequences:

*'It wasn't just irritating, it was infuriating. Can you imagine what it is like to be in the middle of a lesson, you are called to the phone, you are completely distracted from your job – and it was nothing horrendous, boy's pranks, couldn't it have waited?'*          (Parent, also a teacher)

More than anything else parents need to feel that they are 'listened to', that what they have to say is respected and not dismissed. This is both on an informal basis and in more structured meetings. Several also want the views of their child to be taken into consideration.

*'Teachers actually talked to me, explained things and they listened to me. I think that was the most important thing – they listened to me.'*

The ability of class teachers and head teachers to communicate skilfully with parents was very varied. Many of the skills that parents refer to as helpful are the interpersonal skills of warmth, empathy and genuineness, both towards their child and towards them.

*'I found that helpful, someone who had a sympathetic ear and understood the difficulties to get children to school on time. It made you more enthusiastic to get them there on time.'*

*'We get on, she can get through to me, she's honest with me and she gets on with my son, she sticks up for him.'*

Parents appeared able to accept that teachers were having a tough time as well when the context of such conversations was supportive and mutually shared.

*'Children with behaviour problems are very frustrating and actually you need to be able to talk, in an open way with humour as well about what a nightmare they can be.'*

In-school communications were also an issue. Some parents commented that although meetings agreed on certain strategies they were not necessarily carried through by everyone who came into contact with the child. This was a particular concern in the secondary school.

*'Education plans have been drawn up in meetings and you are not at all
sure whether or not they have happened in the classroom.'*

Several parents had been upset by others approaching them and felt
schools should take some responsibility for this. Class peers, other staff
and parents of other children were all mentioned as embarking on negative conversations about the child in question.

*'I was getting people coming up to me saying: "Your son's a really naughty
boy".'*

There is also an issue about communication with agencies, especially in
the health sector.

*'I coordinate with the school and (the clinic). I do that myself, they don't do
that with each other. I don't know why the link isn't there but it's just not.'*

## Actions

Parents were often unable to separate out what is supportive for them in
their interactions with schools from what was supportive for their child.
Actions that take account of parents' views of their child are welcome,
especially when the action is related to encouraging the child to develop
positive aspects of him- or herself.

*'She said she was going to be positive with him, that she'd thought about it
and she was going to praise him and give him little certificates and make
him feel good about himself . . . and that was what actually worked and it
worked from the first week.'*

Parents usually value actions that replicate the parenting functions of
care, protection, encouragement and socialisation, including in some
instances appropriate discipline. Positive communication without positive
action is often frustrating for parents. They would usually prefer to maintain a positive dialogue with teachers but find this difficult if actions do
not follow.

*'It was obvious I was going along with everything. I was being helpful,
attending meetings. I wanted to help him and get him sorted out. I wasn't
going up there screaming and shouting at everybody which I could have
done and basically I was getting nothing. I was at a meeting where one of
the teachers was saying there will be extra help for those children who are
going to find the assessments difficult and I put up my hand and said:
"Does that include (my child)?" The teacher went bright red and said: "Oh
no".'*

*'One of the suggestions made by the educational psychologist was: "Can the teacher spend five minutes a day doing something with him?" . . . and she said: "No, I'm too busy."'*

Whatever the reality for that teacher in terms of curriculum demands, what the parent heard was that her child didn't matter.

The ethos of the school is critical – schools who pass on messages to parents that children with behaviour difficulties are not their problem can appear sympathetic but take minimal responsibility.

*'The head teacher said to me: "If you're not happy with the school find another school" and I just think that she thought that that was the easiest option for him to go somewhere else. I thought that that just shows how they are not concerned for his welfare at all.'*

There are also both covert and overt messages about available resources being allocated to asylum seekers or children with greater difficulties. There is a discourse here that may be in danger of becoming common parlance affecting expectations, attitudes and responsibilities.

*'But they can't afford to help him, they have got children with more problems, like those who can't speak English.'*

Parents have often been asked to remove their child, usually without this being part of an agreed, structured response and have resented this 'knee-jerk' reaction in which schools are seen by parents as not taking appropriate responsibility. This also takes little account of the parents' other needs and concerns.

*'If they didn't ring up in the mornings to pick her up (informal exclusion) they'd ring me in the afternoons . . . I'd go and so my record of work doesn't look very good.'*

Responsibility for action is a contentious issue and reflects previous research. The ideal situation is where parents feel that responsibilities are shared and schools are not opting out.

*'It was saying, "This is my responsibility, this is what I'm dealing with as a teacher and I want to share this with you so you are aware." It was also an openness to suggest any different ways or an opening for me to talk about what we are doing at home. It was a two-way conversation.'*

The most unhelpful scenario by comparison is where schools just seem to want parents to take all the responsibility – but do not offer support or guidance as to what might help.

*'Now what am I supposed to be doing? Do you just want me to shout at him and tell him off, because I do talk to him about what he's done – it's not that I laugh it off and just let him get away with it. I do discuss all the things he's been sent home for but I don't know what you want me to do – but they never had an answer.'*

## What do parents see as facilitating their involvement?

First of all parents have to be comfortable to be in the school at all.

*'She made me feel very at ease and very comfortable . . . if you feel you can go into the school and there is that one person who will listen, you've got the basis for a good foundation.'*

For some parents an informal approach was far less intimidating.

*'She would be happy to walk round the playground with me; she didn't necessarily make it feel official like "everything you say to me is going down in the books".'*

Where there are shared views of a child, similar definitions of behaviour difficulties and when the parent does not have to defend their child against a negative barrage of accusations, they are more able to acknowledge the difficulties and participate in joint problem-solving.

*'She wasn't negative about (his behaviour), just accepting one side of his personality and I thought, well, we're working with the same material.'*

*'Her classroom teacher actually said some positives and I thought, wow, that makes a change. They all recognise that she's got a good heart; she really is a loving little girl when she wants to be.'*

Parents need to understand the language that is being used.

*'I sometimes feel a bit sidelined in meetings. I just feel they use all their terms that I don't understand and they know the system more than I do anyway – that's probably why I feel an outsider.'*

They need to feel that someone in school is committed to their child and to be asked questions that value their own parental role and knowledge of their child.

*'They tried to understand him; that was the most important thing to me.'*

*'We felt that as a result of being able to talk to the teachers we were able to put some sort of balance into the situation.'*

It is also helpful if the parents understand the rationale behind school actions and expectations.

*'I didn't have a clue in the beginning – what on earth are these assessment stages? You really need something you can take home . . . if you've got something at home you can look at it confidently, digest it in your own time or you can go back and say: "Well, I've read this but I don't understand, could somebody explain it to me?"'*

Regular pre-planned contact that tries to maintain a balanced view of events helps to maintain parental involvement.

*'(The teacher) would tell me every day what he had been doing . . . and even if he had a bad day it wasn't totally negative . . . she'd always find something good that he'd done which made me feel better.'*

Where there is a genuine sense of sharing, parents feel that the problems become much more manageable and want to be part of everything.

*'I felt very empowered because I knew what was going on. I felt I didn't have all the responsibility – it was shared. When he was in school it was her responsibility and we were sharing it and we didn't feel isolated.'*

## What do parents see as barriers to involvement?

Parents who feel blamed for their child's difficulties are less likely to want to come into school at all.

*'Every time I went in someone would say: "Your son's done this, your son's done this, your son . . ." I was too scared to go upstairs and pick him up from his classroom.'*

This is also true of parents who feel intimidated by the environment. Meetings where parents are outnumbered by professionals may make them feel marginalised and reluctant to contribute.

*'I felt outnumbered by the head teacher, the deputy head teacher, the teacher all sitting there telling me how bad my son is.'*

Where school staff jump to conclusions about what is happening or have an ethos that rejects rather than attempts to include children with difficulties, shared perspectives are unlikely.

*'I felt that they did dislike him and I thought, well, he obviously thinks that . . . so I thought, how can I send him into that situation, he's only 6 or 7 – how can I do that?'*

Labelling children also gives no room for movement as it limits further discussion. Parents are often given little choice but to defend their child. The boy concerned here had no history of difficult behaviour but was involved in a silly prank that had gone badly wrong. No one was hurt but school property had been damaged. His parents made arrangements to come into school to talk about what had happened.

*'We walked into the study and the head teacher immediately said: "I'm just so sorry for you and your husband – you've got a real problem child there" and the second thing he said was "permanent exclusion". Here was this really bright lad who suddenly had this label. Although obviously we got over it, it was a very, very traumatic experience, very upsetting.'*

There are now more stringent regulations in place to limit such exclusions.

A school ethos that also lets others be negative, including other staff, parents and children, affects parents' feelings about themselves and the school.

*'The children were allowed to say: "Guess what your son did today?" It was very humiliating.'*

Schools that take little account of the other factors that impinge on parents' lives such as work, family and health matters not only make it difficult for parents to meet with teachers but may also alienate them.

*'They wanted me to be available at lunchtimes in case he got into trouble, but it was two buses there and back. By the time I got home it was nearly time to go back again.'*

Establishing relationships with parents where they feel safe to talk about their own concerns can make a significant difference to how much they might be positively involved. This parent has not made her literacy difficulties known in school and dreaded being asked to read something in a meeting.

*'I just wish I could read now; it's embarrassing, a grown-up who can't read.'*

## Parent/carer constructs

Parents bring with them to the home–school interaction many different experiences that influence their constructs about themselves, their children, teachers and the education system. Perceptions of schools are based on their own experiences for either themselves or others, their success as learners, their social relationships and their contact with authority figures.

These all contribute to their level of confidence and also to what they want for their own children. Confidence is often boosted and constructs begin to change when parents are given opportunities and encouragement to contribute – when people make an effort to listen to what they have to say. Support from outside agencies often helps with this.

Cultural issues are relevant in terms of families' expectations of school, their parenting role, expectations for their children, knowledge of the system and language issues. Although there was little direct reference to either institutional or individual racism there were indications that cultural differences and needs are not always given sufficient consideration. This is particularly relevant when both teachers and parents have different values and ideas about what 'ought' to be happening. Assumptions and stereotyping can easily turn to misunderstanding and potential conflict.

## Parental expectations of teachers

Parents had different views of teachers but there is a strong focus on what parents see as 'professional conduct'.

*'They should behave in a professional manner which does not include personal bias against a child.'*

This included a consensus that teachers should focus on learning needs as well as behaviour.

*'The English teacher makes a shortened version of whatever he has to do. As he gets better she makes it longer. But he comes home with science homework and sometimes he gets in a paddy. He's got two science teachers and two different science subjects and we're all confused.'*

Parents brought their own understanding of the educational process and often did not understand or approve of the teaching methods used with their own children.

*'The ways they seem to teach kids nowadays, I might be old-fashioned but it doesn't seem the proper way to me.'*

It was valuable to parents to have opportunities to find out more specifically what went on in school.

*'They did an open day when we could spend a whole day with them and see what they did. That was really good, I really enjoyed that and you could help out with the lessons and everything.'*

Parents need to respect teachers and there are examples in these interviews where teachers have presented themselves in ways that are not perceived as 'professional'.

*'The way I see some of the teachers dress. I mean, how can they set a standard for the future generation when some of them look like tramps. I don't think it gains them any respect whatsoever.'*

There was, however, some sympathy for teachers and the difficult job they have to do.

*'I've come to realise that teachers can only do so much and they've got to be professional with it and that's it really.'*

How teachers are trained and the support they need to manage difficult behaviour was also raised by some parents.

*'I met a teacher in tears by my son. She just didn't know how to handle (the disruption) because she was young and fresh out of training college. I felt sorry for her – she needed someone more experienced alongside her.'*

Parents who are relatively new to the country tend to support teachers' views of a situation. This is less so with the second generation, who may be suspicious of potentially unfair treatment.

*'I am in a better position to protect my children than my parents were able to protect me. I wouldn't automatically blame my children for the things they were accused of and the ways in which they were described and just the way teachers interpret body language and everything. In my experience they don't ever give African-Caribbeans, especially boys, the benefit of the doubt.'*

## Parent perspectives on schools and themselves in the school context

Parents are often intimidated by schools, remembering their own educational experiences. It sometimes takes a high level of awareness to break down these barriers.

*'You go into her office and you feel you're back at school. She'd position her desk so that she was behind the desk, you were in front and she was higher than you. And she did tell me I was talking rubbish . . . she'd belittle, she'd make me feel inferior to her.'*

Few parents felt that they had many rights in school, although some had developed greater assertiveness over time and had begun to make demands. Some parents see themselves as having to 'fight' for their children.

*'Often it boils down to who writes the strongest letter or who pushes hardest.'*

Surprisingly, this was less true of the more 'aware' parents who worked hard for schools to regard them as supportive – in order to protect their child and maintain him or her in school.

*'I've been going to the Parent School Association, I've been going to car boot sales . . . It helps maintain your child in school – while otherwise they might be quite willing to get rid of her. They think I'm supporting them but actually it's to support her.'*

Almost all parents, from all backgrounds, had experienced emotionally distressing episodes in school in which they felt labelled, powerless, tearful or embarrassed. Where they had better experiences, it had considerable implications for their confidence, their relationship with their child and their perspectives on school.

*'I was really nervous about going (to a school meeting) in the first place but I'm glad I went and I'm glad it wasn't all bad. There is light at the end of the tunnel.'*

Nevertheless, this 'equality' is seen as in the gift of the school and teachers rather than an entitlement.

*'They are allowing me to be more involved by letting me know what his routine is – I'm allowed to be an equal.'*

Parents see themselves as fulfilling their parenting role, although many of them feel that they lack confidence and skills. They want schools also to fulfil that role *in loco parentis* in terms of meeting the child's needs, responding to him or her as an individual and ensuring that learning takes place. There is surprise and sometimes anger when they do not see that happening.

*'L. was not a good speller and we used to say in the Junior School: "Please could you send home spellings or work for him to do." We never received anything. We tried to address this with them on a number of occasions and they said: "Yes, they would try and contact us through the homework diary" but it still didn't happen. They just didn't do it.'*

Some parents have re-adjusted their expectations of schools and look for less than they did originally.

*'I can always feel angry about certain things but if that's how things are set what can I do?'*

## Parents' constructs of their own role

Parents' own parenting experiences and expectations of both their own role and their children's behaviour are influential factors in home–school interactions. There were clearly differences between families on these constructs of their parental role, particularly in the varying emphases on functions. Some families were confident of their ability to manage their children and felt frustrated when schools were not.

*'He's always been quite hyper you know, but I've found a way of dealing with it and I'm sure they could have found a way.'*

There was more scope for collaboration when parents perceived similarities between their parenting stance and the way teachers were with their child.

*'But there's a couple of teachers who work the way I do – we all have the same way of dealing with things.'*

Anxiety about children is compounded by anxiety about the parental role and the perceptions of others. Several mothers spoke about episodes of depression or feelings of inadequacy. Empowerment within a home–school partnership appears to alleviate this.

*'The positive things at school have given me more confidence with the kids, I think. I try more.'*

Parents from all backgrounds often see themselves as supporters and defenders of their children although the ways they do this differ.

*'I used to have a row with them over the phone because they wouldn't listen to his side of the story and he can't get his words across.'*

## Summary

One of the more optimistic findings of this study is that several parents spoke about negative experiences in the past but more positive ones in recent times. One bad experience also does not mean there is no hope of better home–school interactions in the future. Each experience, however, does impact on parents' expectations and therefore their initial approach or response in a new situation or with a new teacher. Overall junior schools appear to have better relationships with parents of children with behavioural difficulty than either secondary or infant schools. There are specific difficulties with secondary schools but there is also evidence that a strong and sensitive pastoral system does exist in some places. It is the within-school communication and consistency that presents the greater difficulty. Although frustrations remain and situations do not become fully or quickly resolved, many parents in this study felt that there had been times when they had experienced a more positive approach towards their child and that a genuine home–school partnership had existed. The many outcomes for both child and parent of alternative approaches are discussed in more detail in the next chapter.

## References

Burr, V. and Butt, T. (1992) *Invitation to Personal Construct Theory*. London: Whurr Publishers.
Glaser, B. G. and Strauss, A. L. (1967) *The Discovery of Grounded Theory*. Chicago: Aldine.
Kelly, G. (1955) *The Psychology of Personal Constructs*. New York: Norton.
Robson, C. (1993) *Real World Research*. Oxford: Blackwell.
Roffey, S. (1999) 'The home–school interface for behaviour: the views and constructs of parents/carers'. Thesis for Doctor of Educational Psychology, University of East London.
Smith, J. A. *et al.* (1995) *Rethinking Methods in Psychology*. London: Sage.

# CHAPTER 5

# Outcomes

## Introduction

Although anxiety and frustration about children's behaviour in itself cannot be separated from parents' feelings about the situation, overall there is evidence here that different approaches in school have different impacts on related outcomes. Pupil difficulties are not resolved overnight, especially where there are associated special educational needs, but positive school action and home–school collaboration appear to make a difference for the child, help situations to be more easily managed and are supportive to both parents and teachers. The opposite is also true. The quality of home–school relationships and interventions appear to have either a positive or negative spiral effect with potentially far-reaching outcomes for all concerned. Although these are interactive and systemic, issues have been separated out here for clarity. The first overriding issue is partnership itself and responses related to levels of inequality.

## Outcomes for parents

### Addressing the power imbalance

All parents in the study, regardless of background, had become aware at some point of their comparative lack of power in the school situation. For some this was congruent with their past experiences of education and authority but for others it was unexpected.

Professional families, including teachers, found they had the range of positive and negative experiences typical of other families.

*'I found out that a peripatetic teacher had offered to support (my daughter) in the classroom but the head teacher said she didn't need it without any consultation with me.'*

This same parent was experiencing more collaboration at secondary school, but did consider that her background made a difference to how she and her daughter were perceived.

*'It's immensely helpful for my child to have a parent who's a doctor because I think it adds weight and I wonder whether a working class parent would have got the same response.'*

When positive expectations were not realised families found it both confusing and frustrating.

*'We used to feel here we were, two intelligent parents who love our child and want the best for him. Why not just use us? To us it was like cutting off your nose to spite your face. Why not? That would have been supportive. It would have been supportive to have been listened to.'*

Conversely when the aims of partnership appeared to be fostered within a problem-solving model, parents were empowered both within the school and also in their parental role at home.

*'The behaviour support lady tells me what she's written, what she's got out of her meeting with (my son), what she thinks. The teacher then has her input on his behaviour generally in the classroom and we devise a plan for him and say this is what he needs now. This is what we need to be working on in the school, this is how I need to back it up at home. I find I can monitor it myself, stage by stage, as well as the school and I then know what's happening and I know what I'm dealing with and what I need to do, which is really good. It works as a two-way thing. I make a point of seeing the teacher at half past three saying to her: "How has the day been?"'*

Parents used a number of different strategies to redress the power imbalance. Professional families are at some advantage over others in that they have a wider range of strategies to maintain their child in school. They also understand more of the language. In several instances, however, aware of potential outcomes for their child, they adjusted their responses so that they were seen as less critical of the school.

*'We were terrified he'd be excluded, so our job really was to make sure the school felt we were working with them.'*

Parents whose cultural norms hold education in very high regard are at a particular disadvantage in establishing an 'equal' relationship. They tend to believe that 'teachers must be right' whatever the circumstances. The idea of challenging a teacher's view of a situation is not part of their construct of education. This is particularly true of many recent migrant families.

*'I literally took what the school said for granted as gospel. I went by what they were saying and to this day I feel guilty that I failed (my son) – I should have listened to him.'*

Having someone to support parents in meetings, especially people who know about procedures, is often helpful.

*'(The support worker's) presence made a real difference because she was able to ask things I hadn't thought of.'*

*'The only time they give you a good conversation is when the social worker is with you.'*

This parent used the support worker as a buffer so that she could maintain a dialogue with the school.

*'I've just lost patience and I know if I open my mouth I'm going to say something I regret so I talk to (the support worker) and she puts over my views or she'll question things more.'*

Some parents, however, are a little embarrassed by having someone to support them.

*'I feel just hopeless that I need to have somebody there with me who's more intelligent or whatever or more in the knowledge.'*

Families who have fewer strategies at their disposal admitted that they sometimes appeared 'difficult' and aggressive in their response to schools.

*'Most of the time I go up there I'm in a temper because I want to know what's going on. I'm trying to put my own view across and they don't want to listen so I end up screaming and shouting at them.'*

Others made a point of finding out what the policies in the school were and challenging staff on these. This does not always promote good relationships but it makes an impact on the power balance.

*'I told them it wasn't protocol to exclude a pupil without informing the parents – and it wasn't. She changed her practice after that and the next time there was a potential situation she rang me.'*

## Confidence within the school

Parents often feel very much in the dark when their children's initial difficulties are identified.

*'I just didn't know how to handle it. I was getting no support as a parent on that side of things and plus it was the first time I'd dealt with schools.'*

Some parents had learnt what was possible/acceptable by having support workers with them in meetings and this had boosted their confidence.

*'I think as a parent you are intimidated. Gosh, she is the head mistress, dare I say this, dare I do that? But I've grown as a parent . . . I know I can't be bullied and I know I have rights . . . I don't think I would have known you can do this and the other without the support (worker) . . . and you should know the policies from the beginning.'*

How support services operate within school, however, can also undermine parental confidence and increase their sense of isolation and powerlessness.

*'You know it's the support person, class teacher, head teacher and me, mother. Everyone's got their little titles and I'm just mother. I know for a fact that before the meeting they get together to discuss things before I arrive.'*

Over time many parents learnt a great deal and with that came increased confidence. This family had a child with identified special needs.

*'We've become the experts on our child. You also get to know your way around the education system, and you get information and you talk to other parents.'*

Where behaviour was seen as the single or overriding issue, however, parents had less access to support from other families. Many spoke of their sense of isolation. Several mentioned that a support group for parents of children with behavioural difficulties would be helpful.

*'I think that maybe the school could do something for the parents who want to talk to other parents. I think it would be really good for me to talk to somebody who could understand what I was actually going through.'*

For several parents a negative approach and their decreasing confidence meant that they avoided contact as much as possible. The motivation of this parent to support her child in school was initially very high.

*'It got to the point where I was scared to come into school.'*

A positive response, in contrast, increases parental commitment and confidence.

*'She's supportive of me, she sees my side of things. She knows that's impor-tant as well as the school. She knows I'm fair and won't be against the school for the sake of it.'*

## Confidence within the parent role

The different responses parents had in schools often had an impact on their confidence in themselves as parents.

*'From one experience to another I'm a good mummy, I'm a lousy mummy, I'm a good mummy. I think that the things that happen are bound to rub off on the way you think about yourself.'*

The following parent had an older daughter who was doing very well in school. She felt that the infant school had bombarded her with negative messages about her son.

*'I used to think, well, it must be me. They're not taking me seriously, they obviously think I'm not a very good parent. I think it's the school that made me feel that because before I thought I was doing OK.'*

When interventions are being tried in school in collaboration with parents it gives them ideas about what to work with at home.

*'The positive experience in school has given me more confidence with the kids I think . . . anything they try in school I try and follow at home – if it's practical, it's not always. At the moment (my son) is grounded, he's not allowed to play out until I get home from work . . . Yesterday I thought, at last I've found something that works – a little anyway.'*

Families who are handed the entire responsibility for 'the problem' become less confident in their role within school and also in their role as a parent.

*'I don't know what the school wanted from me. I used to say: "What can I do? You know I don't know what to do. I'm doing my part by bringing him to school and you're just sending him home."'*

## Parent–child relationship

Although there are complex interactions affecting the parent–child rela-tionship there is also evidence that the way schools deal with issues may have an impact. Some parents said that their relationship with the school made little difference to how they saw their child. Most of the time they were aware of both sides of their child's personality, their strengths and weaknesses. These parents often expended a lot of effort trying to counterbalance the teachers' negative impressions of their child in the school context.

*'I always feel the same about (my son) because I know what he can do and I know his capabilities. He doesn't always know his capabilities but I do – he can do a lot more than they make out.'*

Many parents feel protective towards their children and bound to defend them.

*'He's my child, I've got to put him first. This system they've got set up, it's not fair and it's not helping him but they are sticking to it.'*

Other parents, however, talked about how their knowledge of their own child was thrown into doubt by messages they received from school.

*'Suddenly you didn't know your child or you doubted if you knew your child any more – it did change our relationship in a kind of a way.'*

Some parents, initially secure in their parenting role and their relationship with their child, found themselves behaving in ways they later regretted. This parent also felt that her authority at home was being undermined.

*'You take it out on the child because you have felt so frustrated, the school have made you feel embarrassed. You don't want to go back, you can't face another day. You come home and take it out on the child. I've found myself apologising to him a couple of hours later. I'll say to him: "I'm wrong, I shouldn't have shouted, I should have listened to you."'*

This mother who felt that the school's attitude was negative both towards her and towards her son also found herself with conflicting feelings as a parent.

*'I used to get very angry with him and beg him not to behave like this. But he was so vulnerable. I did consider keeping him at home because he was getting so distraught.'*

Where there is home–school consistency the child is less able to manipulate situations and this empowers the parent in their role.

*'He knows that what happens at school happens at home too.'*

Where there is limited communication or it happens via the child then this undermines the parent and further damages the relationship.

*'Because we don't have that close communication and things are dealt with my son without me being there, he seems to try and play us off one against the other.'*

Behaviour difficulties in school often impacted on everyone in the family.

*'It puts a strain on your relationship with your child – and also with your partner.'*

Parents looked for ways to help their children cope in school. Sometimes this was guidance to help manage provocative situations.

*'I keep telling him if anybody do anything to him just go to the teacher, don't retaliate back.'*

There was a recognition by some parents that their children also needed help to cope with less than supportive teachers.

*'There is a maths teacher that everyone has a problem with. Now if I was in the situation of a more able child I would demand a different teacher . . . but I'm not doing that. I say to my daughter: "No matter how you feel about this teacher don't get into a confrontation with her."'*

## Outcomes for children

The outcomes for children are particularly complex. The attitudes and skills of teachers clearly make a difference to how children see themselves in school. When good classroom practice is combined with an effective relationship with parents there are positive outcomes all round.

### Behaviour

Behaviour in school either deteriorates or improves. Difficulties rarely disappear altogether but several parents talked about their child becoming 'calmer'. This was often linked to how happy the child was perceived to be in school.

*'For the first time in his life he's happy in school . . . they work very hard to meet his needs and he has calmed down to a degree.'*

*'Things are a lot better and he can talk to the teachers and he does talk to me now. He does get very irate about things but he is a lot calmer.'*

Conversely an unhappy child will often react in ways which may be perceived as bad behaviour.

*'He would scream and have tantrums every day because he didn't want to go to school.'*

*'The teacher used to make comments and things and embarrass him – he felt very angry towards her. He ran home once in a panic.'*

A few families had sought outside help for their child's behavioural difficulties. Individual therapy, however, was not often perceived as having a useful outcome especially in relation to the school context.

*'He has a psychiatrist but I think we do a lot of the linking about how things affect him at school.'*

*'The therapists were very closed about what was happening but it was very damaging for my daughter in that she now won't engage with any caring professional.'*

*'She goes to see a therapist twice a week in the mornings and she's fallen behind.'*

Support for parents, however, had more positive outcomes.

*'The church has got a parenting workshop which I find very helpful.'*

*'Some of the things that have come out of the (family) sessions lately have been a help.'*

Parents often had clear ideas about what was helpful in improving their child's behaviour and what was not. It was rare, however, that their views were elicited or taken into account.

*'I know it's attention he's looking for and he seems to be getting it for bad things so he'll continue to do bad things.'*

*'But I am thinking that if he is naughty outside in the playground what they should do is to tell him that he must sit in the classroom and not have all his playtime.'*

Appropriate behaviour management was also seen by several parents as meeting their child's needs. Parents tended to feel positive towards teachers they perceived as firm but fair.

*'When he started with her she asked for a meeting with me and I thought that was good. I said to her: "Don't give him that inch because he will take that mile with you." She is very strict and I felt that was a good thing. That's what he needs.'*

## Attendance

Engagement with learning cannot occur if the child is not in school or their attendance is sporadic. This was a major concern in two directions: exclusion from school and reluctance to attend. Schools who regularly exclude children as a management tool effectively bar them from the curriculum and immediately alienate parents. For working parents exclusion from school potentially poses a major childcare problem. In the following instance quoted, arrangements had been put in place for such a contingency but in other instances parents had to leave work suddenly. This puts their work and therefore the family income at risk. The added stress is not conducive to good relationships anywhere.

*'If my daughter needs to be removed from school the childminder will go and collect her but that's when my pocket will be hit because I have to pay her for overtime.'*

Many parents in the study expressed anger at children being sent home, or being put on part-time schooling as it threatened their education.

*'They suspend him for a couple of days and sometimes a week . . . I wanted him to get his education, that's all I was interested about, I didn't want him staying home five days a week.'*

The reasons children were sent home were often not considered to be sufficiently serious by parents to warrant such action.

*'A lot of the time he's excluded for little minor things – he spends more time at home than he does at school.'*

Parents were often aware that their child saw the intended sanction as a reward and therefore an ineffective way of changing behaviour.

*'He got sent home one day for kicking a door or something and I thought, he's probably kicking a door because he doesn't like it at school. Isn't there a way they could deal with him, give him lines or extra work or something but keep him at school because he wants to come home.'*

Pupils who are desperately unhappy in school also opt out. This situation also puts caring parents into a dilemma about the best course of action.

*'He didn't like school and I thought it was so sad. He didn't want to go and I didn't like taking him.'*

*'He didn't want to go to school. He was locking himself in the toilet, he was hiding under the bench. He used to get out of bed every morning really sobbing his heart out, saying that all the teachers hated him.'*

Different approaches do lead to different outcomes. The quote below is about the same child.

*'He wants to go to school now which I thought would never, ever happen.'*

Increased motivation to be in school is a great relief to parents.

*'I know he must be happy because if I'm saying you're sick and you've got to stay home and he's saying no, he must go, he must be a happy child and he must feel quite confident in the school now.'*

## Learning

How well their child was learning was a primary concern for virtually all parents in this study even though the main focus in school was often the child's behaviour. Some parents felt the need to convince schools that their concerns about learning were justified.

*'It's a battle, an uphill battle trying to prove there is something wrong.'*

Several had paid for private assessments, not always to good effect.

*'I gave them the piece of paper which said he had learning difficulties and I thought, well, now surely they have to do something to help him . . . and well, they just didn't.'*

The views of several parents in this study replicated earlier research by seeing poor behaviour in school as an outcome of unmet learning needs.

*'He had trouble with learning in primary school but in the last two years of that we worked with him and brought him up. Since he started secondary school we asked him if he found the work a bit more difficult. He said he did but then he said when he asked for help and the teacher explained it, he still didn't understand it . . . rather than try and do what he can, he just sits back and does nothing.'*

Motivation at school for this boy had been rapidly decreasing and his anxious mother had arranged for her son to have some tuition on Saturday mornings at an African-Caribbean Education Centre. The context and outcome were clearly very different.

*'When he comes home he talks about it and especially when they talked about the nine planets. He came home and he could name them all off and you could see the excitement.'*

The climate in the classroom has a big impact on motivation.

*'When there were positive teachers he was more enthusiastic to go to school, more sort of talkative about what he'd done in school.'*

For many secondary school students, parents note significant differences in outcomes for both learning and behaviour between subjects and subject teachers.

*'There are pockets of things that aren't going very well and pockets of things that are going quite well.'*

Many parents, anxious about their child's progress, had explored a wide range of options to get their child's learning needs met.

*'I spent the whole summer teaching him to write his name.'*

*'I pay for two hours' private tuition on Saturday mornings.'*

By the time this situation has arisen parents are not always receptive to well meaning teachers' enquiries.

*'I told the school about this teacher and all they wanted to know was what she is going to teach him. It's not up to them, is it? They won't give him the help so I don't see how it's up to them.'*

When there is positive action for the child there are often positive outcomes for both learning and behaviour.

*'From the first day he came home and he got a big certificate and it worked – he's started reading now, he's started writing.'*

*'Now he's settled down and does the work and he's doing good work for his standard.'*

Although maturity contributes to learning outcomes it is the focus on the child's learning that made this parent feel more positive about what was happening in school.

*'For the whole term he was there, all he could write was one letter, there was nothing else in his book. But in (current school) they make sure he does two good pieces of work in the morning, and then he has his reading to do.'*

## Social inclusion

Parents are also concerned about outcomes for their child in relationships with others. A sense of being 'connected' to school is increasingly regarded as important both in the short term for attainment and in the longer term for social inclusion. The positive primary experience for this child was not replicated in secondary school and his behaviour was deteriorating.

*'He started to improve, started doing things, got involved in football matches. I think when you go to secondary school you're on your own really and that changed things.'*

The experience for the following child, however, was improving.

*'Before in the nursery he didn't seem to have any friends. He played with everyone but they got annoyed with him and he was not accepted in the group. But now he is, yes.'*

Children who are experiencing difficulties with behaviour also often have problems in their relationships with peers which can lead to a downward spiral unless there is pro-active intervention.

*'The children were attacking my daughter. They were getting really aggressive with her because that's what she was doing to them. If she got frustrated and angry she'd lash out – a couple of days later they'd be waiting downstairs at break time to beat her up.'*

When matters improve the spiral moves upwards. This boy was more motivated to learn, achieving academically, had fewer behaviour difficulties and was socially included in the class.

*'Now I think he just blends in with the other kids.'*

## Perceived outcomes for teachers

There is evidence here that where teachers do make the effort to work in partnership with parents, even if that partnership is flawed then there are benefits all round.

*'The main thing is for each other to know what is happening. It is useful to know when she's been disruptive at school because sanctions I put in at home are quite successful in containing her problems at school.'*

Teachers who are open minded towards children and towards parents are more likely to acknowledge progress and respond accordingly.

*'The teachers who know her well have seen the change in her and are more positive towards her.'*

## Summary

Parents have strong feelings about what schools do or don't do on behalf of their child. These range from frustration to anger to expressions of relief and gratitude. No parent in this study appeared to perceive a helpful, sensitive teacher as 'just doing their job' but showed great appreciation for their efforts. It is these teachers who are memorable and to whom parents referred, however far back in their child's history they were involved.

*'For two years she had very committed teachers who focused on her particular needs and I think that made an enormous difference. They recognised her difficulties and were positive and pro-active about it.'*

Relationships are complex and there are many interactions going on within any given situation. There appears to be a spiral of interrelated factors within and across the two systems of school and family that impact on eventual outcomes. Behavioural issues in school are rarely static; change in one direction or another is inevitable. Although children rarely become paragons overnight there is evidence here that points to better outcomes from a more positive approach. Where parents are empowered in school and in their parental role and schools respond to pupils by focusing on needs as much as management, the outcomes for everyone appear to be much more optimistic. A framework for putting this into practice is the subject of the next chapter.

# CHAPTER 6

# Plugging into Partnership: A Framework for Collaboration

The perceived distance between the home and school can lead to interactions between parents and school staff characterised by defensiveness, lack of co-operation and at times open aggression and conflict . . . if a relationship of confidence, friendliness and mutual support has not been previously established such parent–teacher meetings can become a confrontation rather than a dialogue held for the benefit of the child.     (Dowling and Pound 1994: 70)

## Introduction

Whether it is good, bad or indifferent, families and schools have a relationship with each other. Whatever their level of contact it is desirable that they work harmoniously together and especially so when a pupil is presenting with difficulties. Schools and families have very different systems within which they operate and fundamental issues arise when more intensive interactions are required between them. These include the beliefs that underpin perceptions of role and function, conflicting views of the child and his or her needs and the problems of differential power. Joint systems work (Dowling and Osborne 1994), ecosystemic approaches (Upton and Cooper 1990) and soft systems methods (Frederickson 1990) are all intended to throw light on ways in which more constructive conversations might take place.

Many models address the entrenched difficulties that permeate home–school interactions about pupil behaviour. These usually involve the facilitation of an external consultant. By the time an outside agency is called in, however, relationships may be at an all time low. The most difficult part of the consultant's work may be dismantling the negativity that has already arisen (Dowling and Taylor 1989, Miller 1994). Research illustrates there are concerns about what happens at earlier stages in school when consultants are not there to support and/or monitor interactions

(Wolfendale and Cook 1997, Ball 1998). Personality, teacher skills, school ethos and communication are relevant as well as differences in attribution and definition of behavioural difficulties.

The contextual systems model (Pianta and Walsh 1996) highlights how systems are embedded within systems and that over time 'feedback and feed forward' factors influence perspectives and expectations in a ripple effect. Relationships rather than interventions are seen as having the greatest potential for change. A simple example is where a parent, feeling valued by a teacher, may give more positive messages about school to their child, who then becomes more motivated in the classroom. The same theme is the basis of 'family–school climate building' (Weiss and Edwards 1992) where specific practices are introduced to establish a two-way dialogue and collaborative framework. They include classroom family orientations as well as family–school–child consultations.

This chapter builds on the above models by incorporating the views of parents to develop a broad theoretical framework at the home–school interface to address behavioural issues. This encompasses interactions from before identification of difficulties, through initial identification and assessment to action plans, review and monitoring.

## The home–school interface

An interface may be visualised as the point at which two structures or systems meet. There are alternative images for the home–school interface for behaviour. The first is:

- flat – no effort spent in reaching out to the other
- inflexible – individual points of view fight for precedence
- slippery – misunderstandings and/or apathy arise
- subject to individual caprice – the varying attitudes and skills of individuals.

Such systems have no consistent way of tuning into each other and forming an active partnership. In fact, the opposite often happens and relationships break down into either acrimony or perceived apathy. Both teachers and parents enter the dialogue with their own constructs of the child, their role and the context. Perceptions may be based in a number of different realities, including history, self-esteem, anxiety, pressure and priorities. The detail varies with individual teachers and families but Table 6.1 illustrates some of the more common areas of difference. Most parents see their child's difficulties, if they acknowledge them at all, as part of a wider picture. Even though they may be confused as to why the child is

**Table 6.1**   Possible differences between parents and teachers about behaviour in school

|  | Parents' constructs | Teachers' constructs |
|---|---|---|
| **Behaviour** | Part of the child | A problem for the teacher |
| | Needs to be understood | Disruptive to others |
| | Minimal definition, e.g. 'mischievous', 'high-spirited' | Stronger definition and labelling, e.g. 'naughty', 'aggressive' |
| **Response** | A focus on meeting needs | Management |
| | Defending the child | Protecting others |
| **Schools** | Should focus on learning – my child's learning | Should focus on teaching – not have to deal with behaviour problems |
| **Role of the teacher** | To care for the whole child | To impart knowledge – to pupils who want to learn |
| | To keep discipline | |
| | To be professional at all times | Not to be a social worker or counsellor |
| **Role of the parent** | To protect and defend their child | To take responsibility for their child's behaviour |
| | Ensure needs are met | |

misbehaving, parents usually want the focus to be on their child's needs, whatever they perceive these to be. They may also be anxious not to be 'shown up' by their child and at least for this reason also want school behaviour to improve. Teachers are often focused on the needs of the group being disrupted by poor behaviour as well as the threat to their professional competence. Individual teachers may indeed be very concerned about the welfare of the child in question and structure meetings to try to ensure that the child's needs are acknowledged and met by the parents. The result is likely to be the same. When each side of the home–school interface is fighting for their own perceptions to be heard and accepted there is the possibility of entrenchment, polarisation and negativity.

The teacher who spent half of her precious Sunday going through school files to 'build up a case' to persuade parents that their child was a serious behavioural problem may have been well intentioned but was not making good use of her time. At the Monday morning meeting, faced with a long list of misdemeanours, the parents were left with little option but to defend their child, creep away in embarrassment or blame the school. They may well have been angry, ashamed or depressed but more on account of how they felt labelled as 'failing parents' rather than in sympathy with the teachers. If the aim of the meeting was to encourage parents to work with the school in resolving the difficulties there was a need to go about this a different way.

## *An alternative interface*

There are many schools and individual teachers who do reach out to parents, tune into their perceptions, needs and concerns and share responsibility for problem definition and solution. This 'plugged-in' interface is more flexible, sensitive, responsive and, most importantly, harnesses the power of parents to support the school in effecting positive change. Where this happens parents are often enabled to shift their own thinking so that they can acknowledge difficulties and be more open to working together. It does not happen overnight but there are strong indications that a mutually supportive interaction is possible even with the most 'difficult' parents when certain conditions are in place.

## A theoretical framework for interaction

A theoretical framework for interaction is shown in Figure 6.1. Thought underpins action. There are two major conceptual bases that determine a school's or teacher's willingness and ability to develop positive interactions on behalf of children with behavioural issues. The first is the construct of the child and his or her behaviour and the second is the construct about the place of parents within the school.

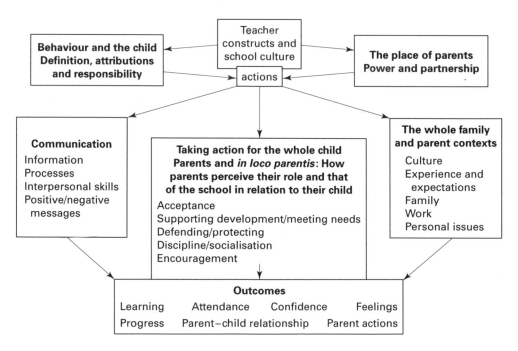

**Figure 6.1** A theoretical framework for interaction

## Pupil behaviour

### Attribution

The thinking about behaviour and reasons given as to why certain behaviours occur are integral to relationships with parents when difficulties
arise. Teachers who do not jump to conclusions, do not blame poor parental management or lack of care, nor label the child, are at a strong advantage in establishing positive liaison. Parents who feel blamed, or expect to
be blamed, may have low confidence in themselves both at home and at
school. This often leads to minimal participation, avoidance of contact or
angry denial. A focus on within-child deficits also leads to a sense of helplessness and potentially negative interactions. Interactive, ongoing assessment *related to a shared view of the whole child* is more likely to encourage
a positive home–school dialogue. To prevent a downward spiral ending
in entrenched difficulties for both the child and the family–school relationship the earlier this happens the better.

There is no doubt that some children come to school with a range of
experiences that are not conducive to generating good school behaviour
and that others have innate or developmental difficulties. What happens
in school, however, either exacerbates or inhibits poor behaviour. Where
schools acknowledge this there is more chance that parents will be willing
partners to a joint approach.

### Definition

What is and is not considered to be a problem often differs between home
and school. Parents may not have the same perspective of difficulties as
teachers and find it hard to accept that their child is unmanageable.
Children who are uncooperative in the classroom may be considered by
parents to behave acceptably at home. Simple descriptions of observable
behaviour, rather than loose labelling terminology such as 'rude and
abusive', is a more useful way of reaching an understanding. Most behaviour has contexts in which it is more or less appropriate – what might
be fine on the football field with mates is not in the classroom with teachers. Discussion of contextual factors may be helpful and also a focus on
actual behaviour rather than labelling children. Talking about different
definitions also offers opportunities to ask parents how they manage their
children and to discuss sanctions that can and cannot be used in the
school context.

## *Taking responsibility*

Management of difficult behaviour is always going to be a primary concern for a teacher. If, however, the focus is on the whole child whose behaviour is giving cause for concern rather than on the 'problem', this provides a mutual reference point for discussion. Partnership is fostered where meeting the child's perceived needs is integral to the school's perspective and they take appropriate responsibility for doing so. Schools who give the impression that help is only available from outside or that resources will have to be taken from other children put families in a vulnerable and powerless position. Although there are pupils who do require external support the first level of responsibility for action belongs to the school. Parents do not always know that they have a right to ask what the school has done and how interventions have been recorded, monitored and reviewed.

## The place of parents

On the one hand there is overwhelming acknowledgement of the importance of parental support (e.g. Sammons *et al.* 1995). On the other there is little room for equality as it is schools who clearly determine the 'partnership' agenda. Schools invariably see themselves as having decision-making power, resource power, position power (with expertise and status) and information power (Vincent 1996). It is therefore up to schools to take the initiative in establishing a culture in which positive interactions with *all* families are viewed as central to optimal effectiveness. It requires a concerted effort to address these issues in a real way if they are not to remain at the level of lip service. Being positive and non-judgemental with some families might be seen as a tall order but appropriate professional interactions need to apply in all circumstances, whatever the provocation to be otherwise. Parents who are struggling with their role also need support not condemnation. Many do not know what to do for the best or have trouble seeing and meeting their child's needs. Working on issues together appears to strengthen parents' own ability to care for and manage their children at home.

The elements of partnership highlighted by parents include the following:

- acknowledgement and value given to parents' complementary knowledge
- full access to equal, accurate and regular information
- working practices that are not conditional, threatening or make unnegotiated demands
- respectful meetings which actively facilitate participation

- seeking a shared perspective of the whole child
- joint decision-making and action-planning in which both parent contexts and teacher responsibilities are taken seriously.

Moving towards partnership can be a challenging professional process since it requires relinquishing some authority in order to move closer to collaboration. It also requires a high level of intra- and interpersonal skills. Teachers who understand the interplay of their own emotions in situations and can make good judgements about their expression are better placed to interact effectively. Taking appropriate responsibility without taking things personally shows professional integrity.

## Communication

Many messages, both direct and indirect, are received by families. These have a powerful impact on how parents see and feel about themselves and their children in the school context (see Figure 6.2). People strive to make sense of what is going on by interpreting communications on the basis of their existing understanding. Where new experiences challenge old constructs there is initial confusion and then the possibility of adaptations in perception and expectation. The existence of strong emotions, however, especially anxiety, may inhibit new learning. Even where schools are being positive parents may hold firmly on to their existing, possibly unhelpful, constructs unless measures are taken to enable them to feel more at ease in the school situation. Parents may then be able to consider alternative perspectives and participate in joint problem-solving. The affective elements of home–school interactions therefore need to be taken into account.

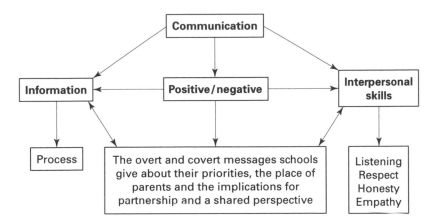

**Figure 6.2** Communication

## Information

Parents' own school experiences and life in the classroom for their own children may be very different and this means that they are at a disadvantage in discussions. A better understanding of the everyday world of their child in school goes some way to redressing the power imbalance. The expectations that are on pupils and the rationale for the approaches taken need to be explained in ways that parents can relate to. 'Orientation' visits and videos of classroom activities have been helpful for some families. Some parents have found that having access to policy documents has also given them a more meaningful say in what happens for their child. This is especially true of special needs and behaviour policies. They need this information to be accessible, given at the outset and translated into community languages.

Information is a two-way process and parents are often able to share things that are helpful to schools in understanding a child's difficulties. They may not, however, trust schools or want to divulge what they consider to be personal, especially where they see schools as 'authority' institutions. They may anticipate assumptions will be made about their family, perhaps be fearful that confidences will be broken – sometimes with potentially far-reaching consequences – or they may simply consider they have a right to privacy. It takes time to develop a relationship in school that allows parents to feel safe in talking about personal matters that affect their children. It is unlikely to happen at all where a parent feels they will be judged. Although such information may throw light on to a child's behaviour this needs to be treated with great sensitivity and only passed on with permission.

## Process

Parents are most interested in what is happening in school for their own child. How information is shared, however, is a central issue. Informal, two-way contact with opportunities to chat about concerns is valued along with regularity of contact that is seen as indicative of a positive ongoing relationship. This contact can be maintained by telephone but only with prior agreement. Phoning can otherwise be intrusive. Privacy is also important. Conversations about behaviour that happen in front of other parents or children can lead to embarrassment and/or anger.

Accuracy of information is not necessarily straightforward. Schools need to ensure that 'facts' are neither hearsay nor unverified opinions. When a child develops a reputation for certain behaviours it is easy for teachers, other staff and pupils to assume blame quickly in any given incident.

Teachers and others do not always realise how specific their 'professional' language is and how often they use shorthand terms with each other. This effectively bars 'outsiders' from participation in meetings. Clarity in giving information, either about procedures or about individuals, enables many parents who would otherwise feel confused or de-skilled. Few have the confidence to ask, fearing to appear 'stupid'. This is particularly important for those unfamiliar with their child's education system as well as the English language. Being given things to read in a meeting does not facilitate partnership, as parents are rarely able to concentrate at such a time or may have literacy difficulties.

It is good practice routinely to ask parents and/or carers to invite someone along with them, especially to larger meetings. Being alone can be very intimidating, Having a friend or parent supporter there reduces feelings of being outnumbered by school staff, provides psychological support, gives greater opportunity for asking questions and opportunity to talk things over with someone afterwards. If no childcare facilities are available it also helps share the care of smaller children.

### In-school processes

Parents need to know that what has been agreed in a meeting will apply for their child throughout the school. In secondary schools pupils come into contact with many different teachers and in primary schools there are lunchtime supervisors and perhaps temporary teachers. A whole-school approach that clarifies communication processes is more likely to promote consistency in carrying through agreements and action plans. This also highlights the need for good recording and monitoring so that parents do not have to feel that they are 'back to square one' when new staff take over.

## Interpersonal skills

Good interpersonal skills are facilitated by high levels of self-awareness. Teachers who are able to interact in a consistently skilled way have more chance of eventually establishing interactions that are of benefit to the child.

### Listening

Being listened to, having their views heard and taken into account is far and away the most important interpersonal skill that parents value. They want to be taken seriously and not dismissed or labelled, let alone blamed. They would like teachers to be non-judgemental, not make assumptions,

**What is involved in listening to and hearing parents?**

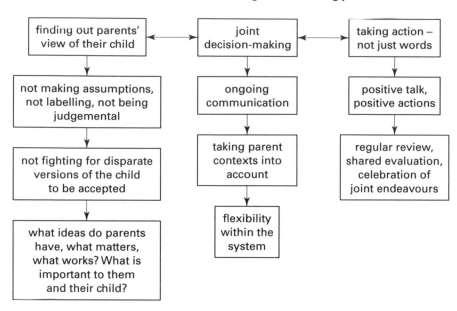

*Listening to expressions of feelings is as important as the words*

**Figure 6.3** What is involved in listening to and hearing parents?

find out from them what they think and then use this information in planning for the child. Many parents consider they have something useful to offer to the situation but in many instances this is neither sought nor valued in a constructive way. The circumstances and atmosphere of meetings might inhibit parents from saying anything at all, for fear of being thought stupid or ignorant (see Figure 6.3).

### Respect

Although respect has much to do with listening as outlined above, there are other issues that have been mentioned by parents. Where formal meetings are required these need to be organised properly in advance and begin and end on time. Being kept waiting, especially without explanation and apology, devalues parents' efforts to be there. It is important that relevant people are enabled to attend, that parents are introduced to anyone they do not know and that the same information is available to everyone. Constant interruptions by others, either in person or on the phone, gives parents the impression that they are not being properly listened to and that other matters have a higher priority. A sign on the door and a phone off the hook helps. Seating arrangements and how individuals are addressed also needs to promote equality.

### Honesty

Parents value honesty – they do not want to be misled or patronised in any way. There is, however, a proviso that honesty is based in a shared perception of the child that also acknowledges strengths. Unrelieved negativity is not welcome. Parents do, however, want expectations that are more or less realistic so that they don't feel let down when things do not materialise. Honesty from teachers which acknowledges they don't always know what to do for the best or get things wrong sometimes is also helpful.

### Humour

Some parents welcome a more light-hearted sharing about how dreadful a child can be – but such an approach has to be initiated by them or at least handled with great sensitivity. In the first instance, parents need to be assured that they are being taken seriously.

### Empathy

The expression of empathy also requires a high level of skill. Acknowledging feelings validates them and emphasises that what parents think and feel matter. A teacher telling a parent 'I know just how you feel' can, however, backfire, especially if the parent's circumstances are particularly complex and difficult. Empathy is more likely to be considered genuine if there is a warmth and willingness with actions as well as with words.

### Specific skills needed in difficult situations

Although teachers sometimes find themselves in situations in which parents are confrontational, the guidelines above still apply. Where parents are overtly hostile teachers need to maintain a physical distance, not move suddenly and speak quietly. This portrays an appropriately assertive but non-threatening stance. It is wise to have other people in the interview. If a parent is in a high emotional state then attempting to reason with them is unlikely to be successful. Mirroring anger will exacerbate it. It is better to acknowledge distress and, if possible, either give parents an opportunity to calm down in a quiet place or make an arrangement to see them at a later date.

## Negative/positive approaches

Negativity is a major concern in some schools and has far-reaching consequences for partnership as well as the amelioration of behaviour difficulties. Consistent negative messages about a child are very distressing and affect parents' feelings about themselves, their children and the school. When a negative approach is encountered the parents' view is that it is often all-pervasive, raising questions about school ethos and management as well as the perceptions and skills of individual teachers. It makes the parent feel defensive and helpless in the school situation and may make them reluctant to meet with school staff. It is not only teachers who are responsible for messages about children but also other staff, other parents and children. Such negativity needs to be addressed at a whole-school level. It takes sophisticated skills in parents to tackle negativity in their efforts to work with the school to support their child and many are simply unable or unwilling to do so. When parents hear positive things said about their children and positive actions taken by teachers, such as issuing 'success' certificates, it makes a great deal of difference in raising confidence and improving relationships. Qualifying small improvements by saying things like 'if only he could always do this' detracts from the positive message. Positive letters home are also very powerful both for the child and for the parent.

## The whole family: parent contexts

The world that parents inhabit contains not only their children but all the other aspects of their lives. Many parents are trying to juggle many demands upon them, including work and family commitments, health issues, differences with their partners over management of the child and other emotional tensions. Schools need to take sufficient account of these contexts. It is easy to blame parents for apathy or lack of commitment when there are many other reasons for reluctance or inability to engage. Parents will be more likely to attend meetings if these can be arranged at times that are mutually convenient, in a language that the parent understands and when all their other responsibilities are respected. Sometimes the option to meet at home might be welcomed.

Parents do sometimes have other priorities and judgements may be made on these if they are different from the school's. Asking parents what they can manage and are willing to do sets up more realistic expectations of involvement, rather than schools deciding and parents theoretically going along with this.

Many single parents in particular are put under great stress when they are constantly called into school or expected to be at home to supervise their 'excluded child'. Schools may not always realise the consequences of their actions for the whole family, including the potential or actual loss of earnings.

Parent contexts also refer to the experiences and expectations underlying parental constructs. Many of these are linked to their own memories of school and in some cases their continuing contact with authority figures. The feelings engendered by these constructs may be powerful and determine how parents view themselves in relation to school personnel. This in itself may be a barrier to partnership until there is an account taken of the feelings that parents bring with them and an effort made to demonstrate the value and respect given to their current role in school. Some parents may take offence at innocent comments if these revive painful memories. It isn't possible to know this but may help to understand a response that may initially appear irrational.

Cultural contexts impact both on behaviour and on the home–school interface. These are covered more fully in other chapters in this book. Schools that wholeheartedly value diversity will not make judgements or assumptions about families but seek to understand their constructs, values and expectations in order to facilitate partnership.

## The whole child: parental role and *in loco parentis*

In the great majority of cases, what is supportive for children is supportive for parents. Good relationships on their own are not sufficient to maintain positive home–school interactions; actions in school need to follow. Parents talk about their levels of frustration when there is no tangible difference in what happens in school following discussions.

When parents meet with teachers they are concerned about two interconnected strands of responsibility. The first is their view of themselves as the child's parent and what their interactions in schools mean for the fulfilment of this role. Will they have to defend or protect their child or attend to his or her learning needs? The way teachers talk about the child makes a difference to the manifestation of this role. A barrage of negativity, for instance, may mean that a parent has to 'stand up' for her child, even in the face of what the school may see as damning evidence. If the parental role, however, has a far stronger focus on discipline and the cultural norms for the family dictate that teachers are always right, then the child may be punished at home as a result of the discussion – not necessarily the intended outcome.

The second strand is that parents value and will work with teachers who are able to share their perceptions and understanding of the whole child and mirror their parenting role and concerns in school. Positive home–school interactions follow where teachers have been able to convey a genuine concern for the child and acknowledge positive aspects as well as difficulties. Parents prefer honesty about their child and in these circum-stances are able to share both the anxieties and the frustrations. Many parents have a focus on learning outcomes for their child and are re-assured when there are structured, positive activities in school to promote this.

Parents who are, however, struggling to fulfil their basic parental func-tions need support to do so. Unless schools also take on some appropri-ate *in loco parentis* responsibility here the child is left without an advocate and their behaviour difficulties will inevitably exacerbate.

## Parenting functions

Wolfendale (1992) refers to parenting functions and styles that differ according to culture and may be subject to judgements by others. Cultural expectations impact strongly on the home–school interface as families emphasise different aspects of their role. There are, however, cross-cultural universals as well as culturally specific features in child rearing practices. All children are, for instance, seen as learners, and this is a feature of the parent–teacher role that could be a starting point for any interaction.

### Supporting development

Parents see school as the place where their child goes to learn. Achievements are therefore at the forefront of their mind when they meet with any teacher. Parents may be very anxious about their child's progress and it may be better to begin the conversation with what their child has been able to do, however little this is, rather than a long list of their fail-ures. This reduces initial anxiety and will enable parents to participate more fully in discussing ways forward. Parents may have other concerns such as transition between classes or social relationships. Asking parents about their concerns and involving their ideas in planning ways of meeting these in school show that they are being taken seriously. Parents will usually be willing to consider behavioural issues as part of further planning.

It is possible that some parents feel that their child's needs have been neglected through delays in putting anything in place. They may arrive to meet with a new teacher angry or disillusioned because of these past expe-riences. This again highlights the importance of good recording. Some parents see their parenting role as one on one and want this replicated in school. When this is not appropriate or possible, parents need to know what is happening instead and how that is being monitored.

## Acceptance

Theoretically, all teachers are expected to take responsibility for all children with special educational needs, including behavioural needs. The reality is that schools often feel that they do not have the resources to 'cope' with a high level of demand when pressure is on them to achieve high academic results. The outcome in some schools is that children who present with time-consuming needs or undermine a teacher's pedagogic efforts are quickly encouraged to be 'someone else's responsibility'. Whether this responsibility is foisted on to support services, alternative educational provision or parents, the message that parents receive, however inadvertently, may be 'your child doesn't belong here'. The sense of rejection can be acute and generate considerable hostility. Where schools take their responsibilities for inclusion seriously they are more likely to focus on the possibilities and generate positive actions. There is also less need for crisis management. The parental role of acceptance also means they want others to see their child as a whole person who, despite their difficult behaviour, also has positive qualities. It is sometimes the case that parents are rejecting their child. For the school to do so also will invariably exacerbate the child's emotional and behavioural difficulties.

## Defending/protecting

When faced with a barrage of accusations against their child, parents will often see their role as an advocate. They may not be able to hear what teachers are trying to say is the 'reality' of the situation. They may blame the school, other pupils, teacher bias or unmet needs. Parents with this perspective value highly those teachers who they see as supporting and 'sticking up for' their child. Pupils with behavioural problems often have poor peer relationships and parents want schools to have policies and effective practices that protect their child from bullying, ridicule and derogatory labelling.

## Socialisation and discipline

For some families this is one of the more important parental functions. In school this means that they want strict teachers who maintain good discipline in the classroom and are able to 'manage' difficult behaviour. Discussions about behavioural expectations, rewards and sanctions help parents to understand how schools are attempting to do this. Parents often want good communication to ensure that their child is not able to manipulate situations between home and school.

Some children may not have had the opportunity to learn appropriate social skills and therefore teaching and reinforcing 'good school behaviour' at the outset will be worthwhile.

If the family's overriding emphasis is on discipline it may be important that the other *in loco parentis* functions of care and encouragement are in place in school.

### Encouragement

This is linked to the 'negative/positive' communication outlined above. Where teachers focus on strengths, self-esteem and actively promoting success it not only reassures parents, but also gives them ideas of approaches to try at home. A pupil who has targets that are unreachable, however, will be discouraged and stop trying. The same is true of an older student who has no say in the targets that are set. Parents need to understand the rationale behind what schools are trying to do, so that everyone's expectations are appropriate. Everyone makes mistakes and fails from time to time. Parents, teachers and students need to acknowledge that this is part of the learning process.

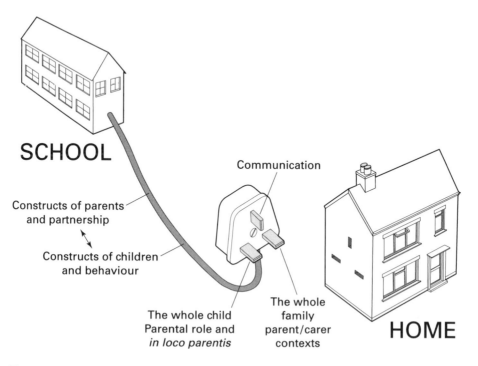

**Figure 6.4** The plugged-in interface

## Summary

The way teachers think about children with behavioural difficulties and the way they think about parents affect the way they communicate, the actions they take on behalf of the child and their ability to take account of issues that impinge on parents' ability to work with the school (see Figure 6.4). Although the views of individual teachers are of great importance, so too is the ethos of a school and the culture that supports it. This can be summarised by the way the school 'lives' its values in the conversations and other communications that take place, the actions that are encouraged and the views people have of their responsibilities to the pupils, the parent community and each other.

## References

Ball, M. (1998) *Disabled Children: Directions for their future care*. Wetherby, Yorkshire: Social Care Group, Department of Health and the Council for Disabled Children.

Dowling, E. and Osborne, E. (eds) (1994) *The Family and the School: A joint systems approach to problems with children*. London: Routledge.

Dowling, E. and Taylor, D. (1989) 'The clinic goes to school: lessons learned', *Maladjustment and Therapeutic Education* 7(1), 24–8.

Dowling, J. and Pound, A. (1994) 'Joint interventions with teachers, children and parents in the school setting', in Dowling, E. and Osborne, E. (eds) *The Family and the School: A joint systems approach to problems with children*, 69–87. London: Routledge.

Frederickson, N. (1990) 'Systems approaches in educational psychology practice: a re-evaluation', in Jones, N. and Frederickson, N. (eds) *Refocusing Educational Psychology*. London: Falmer Press.

Miller, A. (1994) 'Parents and difficult behaviour: always the problem or part of the solution?', in Gray, P. *et al.* (eds) *Challenging Behaviour in Schools*, 92–107. London: Routledge.

Pianta, R. C. and Walsh, D. J. (1996) *High Risk Children in Schools: Constructing sustaining relationships*. New York: Routledge.

Sammons, P. *et al.* (1995) *Key Characteristics of Effective Schools*. London: OFSTED and London University Institute of Education.

Upton, G. and Cooper, P. (1990) 'A new perspective on behaviour problems in schools: the eco-systemic approach', *Maladjustment and Therapeutic Education* 8(1), 3–18.

Vincent, C. (1996) *Parents and Teachers: Power and participation*. London: Falmer Press.

Weiss, H. M. and Edwards, M. E. (1992) 'The family–school collaboration project: systemic interventions for school improvement', in Christenson, S. and Coneley, J. C. (eds) *Home–School Collaboration: Enhancing children's academic and social competence*, 215–43. Silver Spring, MD: National Association of School Psychologists.

Wolfendale, S. (1992) *Empowering Parents and Teachers: Working for children*. London: Cassell.

Wolfendale, S. and Cook, G. (1997) *Evaluation of Parent Partnership Schemes*. DfEE Research Report Number 34. London: The Stationery Office.

## CHAPTER 7

# Working with Parents Who Harm Their Children

*Anna Harskamp*

---

### Case study: Darren

Darren was 12 years old when, in counselling, his mother made the link between her negative feelings about him and her physically and emotionally abusive behaviour towards him. She had experienced her own mother as harshly punitive and, at Darren's age, was frequently locked in a room with bars at the window and no light bulb in the room. Of her four children, who were all boys, Darren, the second eldest, was the only one she abused. He reminded her of his biological father who left her in mid-pregnancy. A few hours after she had given birth to Darren, she heard his father's voice in the hospital ward. He was visiting his new partner and their baby daughter who, coincidentally, had been placed in a bed opposite to Darren's mother. She described feelings of hatred for Darren emanating from that time.

Intensive multi-agency interventions with Darren and his mother by the social worker, school staff and therapeutic staff led to a position where Darren and his mother were able to develop a more appropriate relationship which ceased being hostile and abusive. As Darren's mother put it: 'The ice I always had had in my heart for him started to thaw.'

---

### Introduction

This chapter will focus on working effectively with parents who have harmed their children and where there are concerns regarding the behaviour of these children at school.

In this chapter, 'parent' will be taken to refer to any adult who has direct care responsibilities for the child. As well as parents this can also refer to step-parents, other family members who have parental responsibility, a parent's partner, foster carers and others.

It is important to state at the outset that the safety and welfare of the child must always remain the priority concern. This is documented in international as well as national legal frameworks. The United Nations Convention on the Rights of the Child (Anonymous 1993) enshrines the rights of children and young people to:

- protection from violence and harmful treatment (articles 19 and 37)
- protection from exploitation, which includes sexual abuse (article 34).

These rights apply to all children whatever their race, religion, gender, language, disability or family background (article 2). Decisions that affect children should be made in the best interests of the child (article 3) and the views, thoughts and feelings of the child should be listened to very carefully (article 12).

The rights of children are also being articulated at the same time that parental duties, rights and responsibilities are becoming more prominent, particularly in the field of education. Research on pupil achievement and school improvement highlights the value and importance of parental views and support. Hallgarten (2000) outlines the justification for parents having a voice in the educational system and describes six ways in which this voice can be expressed:

1. Silence, such as inaction, non-articulation, waiting and seeing
2. Informal conversation, such as engaging with the system
3. Formal deliberation, such as writing or meeting formally
4. Storming – protesting against the system
5. By-pass – going around the system or making own arrangements
6. Exit, which refers to the child leaving school or abandoning the system.

When we are trying to understand the factors that lead to a parent harming or abusing their child, it can be very difficult to think about giving the parent 'a voice'. As Buchanan (1996) states in her work on cycles of child maltreatment: 'There is an instinctive need to pathologise and marginalise the abuser.' The notion that a parent can perpetrate abuse against their own child, sometimes of the most awful and damaging kind, can feel deeply disturbing. It goes against our sense of and desire for the family being the place where children should be safe and cared for. These feelings need to be expressed safely by teachers and other key staff working in schools with children who have experienced abuse at the hands of parents. Parents may also bring strong feelings into school with them.

Some will have highly negative views of their own schooling and of key people that they met within school. Others may associate their school days with traumatic events that happened to them at the time. Parents may also be highly aware of the power relationships that can exist within a school system. This chapter will examine ways of understanding and thinking about the complexities of abuse, appropriate channels for staff to express feelings and ways to develop strategies for action. Education professionals need to know how best to respond to both the parent and the child in the interests of the child.

## What does 'significant harm' mean?

Jamie was 6 years old when he was referred to the educational psychologist because of behaviour described by his teachers as extremely aggressive – both to children and to adults. He was hitting, kicking and spitting at others and seemed a very sad, isolated child. Jamie was under-functioning at school. He drew a picture of himself completely surrounded by what he called a 'force field' to 'protect' him.

The 'protection' that Jamie felt he needed was to minimise the pain he felt from his mother's beatings with both a belt and her hand. The complexity of the relationship he had with his mother was shown by his description that not only did the force field protect him but it also protected his mother's hand from getting 'too hurt'. Children abused by their parents will not infrequently express the sort of emotions such as, 'I love my mum but I want her to stop doing that.' Jamie's mother also needed a great deal of help, from a number of sources. She had to come to terms with how she felt about her relationship with her son, learn what else she could do when she felt angry, hurt or let down by his behaviour and how she could allow him to be 'just a child'.

In the UK, the concept of 'significant harm' was introduced with the Children Act 1989 (DoH 1989), as the threshold that justifies compulsory intervention in family life. There are four types of child abuse or maltreatment which may occur together or separately. Emotional abuse is a component of all the other types of abuse:

- physical abuse
- emotional abuse
- sexual abuse
- neglect.

The impact of abuse and neglect on children can be profound and long term. Aspects of a child's health, development and well-being may be affected. Interpersonal and social difficulties may be apparent as well as issues about self-esteem, self-image and self-worth. Learning may become seriously affected as a child feels they are 'too stupid' to learn effectively. Consequently academic and linguistic achievements may be negatively affected. Detailed definitions of abuse and the impact of abuse are given in Working Together to Safeguard Children (DoH 1999) and Harskamp (1996).

There are no absolute criteria of what constitutes significant harm and the following factors should be considered:

- the severity of the ill-treatment
- the degree and extent of physical harm
- the duration and frequency of abuse and neglect
- the extent of premeditation
- the degree of threat and coercion
- sadism or unusual or bizarre elements in sexual abuse.

The extent to which children can be significantly harmed should be seen as a function of a number of factors including:

- the family context
- the child's development within the context of their family and wider social and cultural environment
- any special needs, such as a medical condition, communication difficulty or disability that may affect the child's development and care within the family
- the nature of harm, in terms of ill-treatment or failure to provide adequate care
- the impact on the child's health and development
- the adequacy of parental care.

It is always important to take account of the child's reactions and his or her perceptions according to the child's age and understanding (DoH 1999).

## What are the sources of stress for children and families?

Parents in many families under stress, even severe stress, do not abuse or harm their children. The sad reality, however, is that some do. It is important to try to tease out and understand some of the factors that can lead to further stressors for parents, which may exacerbate already difficult situations. It is also important to try to maintain a non-judgemental stance with regard to some of these factors that may affect a parent's capacity to keep their child safe from harm. It is apparent that individuals and families have different strengths and coping mechanisms and that what will bring one parent to crisis may barely impact on another. There is a very complex interplay of factors involved in this whole area and a great deal of care needs to be taken in understanding what the impact of various parental or family stresses could be on an individual child or children (Cleaver *et al.* 1999).

---

## Case study: Simone

Simone was 8 years old and was described by her teacher as a worrying and worried child who was isolated from her peers. She rarely smiled and would not communicate with her teacher anything to do with home. She was said to find it difficult to remember what she had learnt from one day to the next. She appeared to be overwhelmed by school and its routines. She was an only child who lived with both parents. She was always brought to school and picked up by her father, who, the teacher reported, was always hurrying from or to his workplace.

By building up a relationship with Simone's father, over time, her teacher was able to understand the huge stresses the family were under. She was able to help the family seek appropriate support at home by linking up with other key agencies. She was also able to understand Simone's situation more fully and with sensitive approaches and support, Simone was able to start slowly to trust people and to make more sense of school.

Simone's mother was receiving treatment for a serious psychiatric condition, which included her having hallucinations at times. She was often in bed during the day and evening. At other times she would seem fine. Simone's father worked nights and often had to work overtime to help the family cope financially. Simone had experienced neglect while she was technically under the care of her mother while her father was working. From a very young age Simone had been left in the care of an adult who was mentally ill, at times acutely so, and whose behaviour she could not understand, or predict, or trust.

---

Sources of stress for children and families may include the following:

- **social exclusion** – crowded or unsuitable accommodation, financial problems, racial harassment
- **domestic violence** – which can impose physical as well as psychological threats for the child and family

- **mental illness** of a parent or carer – may blunt a parent's reactions to a child or cause them to react in an unpredictable way
- **drug and alcohol misuse** – risks will be greater to the child when the parent's addiction and behaviour are chaotic or lead to criminal involvement.

Other aspects of parental behaviour or experience may lead to further risks for the child. In all such cases it will be essential for a thorough multi-disciplinary assessment in order to assess the degree of risk to the child and to plan positive ways forward. Social services would normally be the agency to lead on this.

## The essential context of school and the vital importance of the teacher

Attendance at school provides a universal service for children and young people in 'developed' countries. Each child has access to a teacher, or several teachers. Where children with special educational needs are included in mainstream school, support staff may be working directly with children. 'All those working in the education services can contribute to the safeguarding of children and the child protection processes' (DoH 1999). There should be local, school and national procedures to enable worries about actual or possible child abuse to be dealt with effectively. The reasons for teachers becoming involved with child protection vary. The teacher may have noticed worrying indicators of abuse or neglect in the child or a child may have made a direct allegation about being abused. Sometimes a parent may disclose that the child has been or is being abused. Sometimes the abuser being referred to is the parent themselves. This may emerge directly or indirectly. For example, a parent may describe the ways he or she punishes the child at home. When these descriptions appear to be harmful or abusive to the child, the teacher will need to act by reporting the concerns to the appropriate person(s) and, wherever possible, directing the parents to suitable support. This scenario is a complex one and raises a number of key issues and questions for the teacher. These may include:

- How do I deal with all of this?
- What do I do about the mixture of feelings going around inside me?
- Who is there to support me?
- What training have I had or will I need to prepare me for this?
- How do I carry on working with this child when I know what awful things have been happening?

- How do I go on working with this parent when I now know some of the awful things this parent has done to harm their own child?
- How can I keep focused on the core fact that the child is in school to learn and I am in school to teach?
- What do I have to do about contact with all these other professionals, most of whom I have never met before?
- How will I know if this child will in any way have benefited or have been safeguarded as a result of my actions?
- Will this parent be helped to learn better ways of dealing with their child?
- What kind of information do I need to have or find out about and what do I have to record?
- What will I have learnt from this experience which will help me next time?

The feelings generated by such situations can be confusing or overwhelming for any member of the school staff directly involved with a child in their class. A teacher might feel sympathy and concern for the child whose behaviour may also be exasperating. The teacher might also feel very angry towards the parent who has harmed the child as well as disgusted by the actual details of the abuse. With some teachers there will also be personal triggers of their own childhood abuse or hurtful or traumatic times. Triggers may be generated by a very wide variety of stimuli and frequently appear almost 'out of the blue'.

The author and colleagues carried out support work at a school, following the abduction of a nine-year-old child. Several staff spontaneously recalled traumatic experiences that had been triggered by this event. For one, it reminded her of experiences and feelings she and her family had had in the war when her father had been reported missing. For another, it was a very painful reminder of her own experience several years earlier when a child had also gone missing. Subsequently this child's body had been discovered buried in the garden of the family home where she had been cruelly tortured, sexually abused and then murdered by her parents. This particular teacher was beginning to feel that, although she knew it was illogical, children she came into contact with somehow had really bad things happen to them. What was important was that both of these teachers were given an appropriate place and time to reflect on these troubling issues.

As Trowell *et al.* (1996) state:

For all of us – however senior and experienced we are – the emotions that are stirred up need a place and some time for consultation and discussion. The principal need is to hold on to the capacity to think, to observe, assess, evaluate and be in touch with the range of feelings; and to go on thinking.

Child protection work must always be properly and professionally supported. Staff can feel very isolated when working in this area and need to have clear mechanisms for support, supervision and guidance. The worst aspects of cases where parents harm their children can 'get under your skin'. There can also be a risk of what has been called 'professional dangerousness', described in the literature as:

- professionals operating alone
- professionals colluding with the family in order to avoid issues or to maintain relationships with them
- professionals acting unsystematically and without a theoretical base
- maintaining unrealistic optimism against the evidence
- becoming over-involved with family members or the family in general
- over-identifying with the family
- being unaware of the importance and strength of personal feelings and values
- avoiding contact because of fear of personal safety. Personal safety issues are very important for all professionals and no undue risks should be taken by any member of staff. Schools should have guidelines relating to personal safety in the workplace and clear strategies that can be used in practical situations.                      (Dent 1998)

Clarity regarding statutory procedures in cases of abuse is vital and a keen awareness of the role and function of each professional in the whole scenario is essential. For example, in the UK, most parents will be invited to child protection conferences where their own abusive behaviour to their child is being discussed. Decisions will be made about whether, for example, to place their child's name on the Child Protection Register.

---

# Case study: Shebana

Shebana was 11 years old and described as having very challenging behaviour with some autistic features. She was also showing very unusual difficulties in learning. At home, her mother, who confided her own learning difficulties at school, despaired at times because she found Shebana very difficult to understand or to deal with. One summer, Shebana and her younger sister and her mother were out in the local park for a special treat. Shebana was, as her mother put it, 'playing up', and in anger, her mother lashed out at her. This physical chastisement of Shebana, by her mother, was reported to the Police by a member of the public who felt that the mother's response had been unusually punitive to the child. Subsequent multi-agency assessments resulted in a child protection conference. Shebana's mother and her partner were in attendance throughout and were able to give a much clearer picture of the kinds of stresses and difficulties the family were under. The incident in the park had been symptomatic of a whole host of mother–daughter relationship problems. Support, of a very practical kind, was offered to the family as well as focused therapeutic input. Shebana's teacher played a key role in planning the child protection pro-gramme, including regular meetings at school with the mother and partner to discuss any issues relating to their concerns about Shebana.

Good quality up-to-date training is very important in enabling teachers to feel skilled and knowledgeable about child protection matters. Access to high quality consultation and support is also essential for the teacher to feel that an effective approach can be made from the school setting. Recent guidance in the UK has led to core groups being set up fol-lowing child protection procedures. These enable those most concerned with the child and the parent to develop a coordinated approach to inter-vention over time. A teacher would normally be an important part of such a core group.

For all of the above there are very clear resource implications for school planning and management, such as the teacher's time.

## The challenge of partnership with parents who harm their children

While many parents can be supported in developing different ways of relating to their children in a non-abusive way, it is a reality that there are some who will not be deemed to be adequate parents. Their children will not, in the child's best interests, be allowed to live with them (see Chapter 8). It is important to state that many parents who themselves experienced punitive parenting as a child will not go on to harm their children. Much research is currently focused on the notion of 'resilience' in children where, despite adverse circumstances, the child is still able to develop self-esteem, confidence and develop appropriately. Protective factors appear to be those that to some extent shield the child from the full impact of adverse circumstances (Buchanan 1996).

Interventions with families have sometimes been referred to as hopeful, doubtful or hopeless. Some of the research which has led to this kind of typology has come from an analysis of child abuse tragedies or extreme cases of abuse perpetrated by parents. Reder and Duncan (1999) in their second study of fatal child abuse cases came up with a number of factors which they felt were relevant to prediction of risk of future harm to children and could alert practitioners:

- parental history of maltreatment, rejection and/or being in the care of a local authority
- unresolved conflicts in the relationship with the parental family of origin
- a violent relationship between the parental couple
- the presence of a mental health problem in either parent, especially when linked with substance misuse and delusional thinking involving the child
- minimal antenatal care
- ambivalence about or rejection of the pregnancy
- the child being attributed with a negative meaning.

The meaning of the child is a profound aspect of the parent–child relationship and can take on negative attributions when, for example, a child is born at the same time as a transitional or traumatic event in the parent's life. (Darren, described at the beginning of this chapter, is an example of this.) Sometimes a child is seen in the image of a poorly regarded or despised member of the family: 'He's violent and aggressive just like his real dad.' A child can also be expected to fulfil an inappropriate role for a parent. A lonely parent looking for love from their baby may interpret the baby's incessant crying as a sign of rejection. In such situations the parent might start to feel even more worthless because they see themselves as unable to parent their own baby. An awareness raising campaign in Newham, East London, in 1996, showed the dangers of shaking babies (Sampson and Shepherd 1996). The highest risk factor for a parent shaking a baby was incessant crying. Such parents, mostly mothers in this case, have been described as motherless or unmothered mothers. They need to feel nurtured themselves in order to parent their own child effectively. These parents have often experienced a past that hurt and still hurts.

Other unresolved conflicts which parents may have are what Reder and Duncan (1999) have called 'care and control conflicts'. This is when a parent's own adverse childhood experiences being parented have left them with unresolved conflicts and stresses that have permeated their adult relationships. These conflicts are about being cared for or caring for others or about control issues, either wanting to control others or wishing to be controlled by them. These conflicts can be interrelated and parenting problems can be seen as the result of difficulties in balancing caring and controlling in the child–adult relationship. Occasionally, a situation arises that is always extremely worrying and that is when it appears almost as if the child does not exist in the parent's world, particularly at a psychological level.

Given the complexity of some of the backgrounds and situations of parents, there is indeed a real sense of challenge in working with parents who have harmed their children. Child protection workers have described a 'ladder of partnership' with parents (Calder and Horwath 1999). This ladder has the following 'steps':

- full participation
- participation
- involvement
- consultation
- keeping fully informed
- no partnership.

For full participation to be achieved there has to be a realistic understanding of a parent's responsibility for the abuse and their capacity and desire for change. The following framework enables professionals and the family themselves to assess where input should be focused. The abusing parent, or parents, needs to address the following:

- I/we accept there is a problem.
- I/we have some responsibility for the problem.
- I/we have some discomfort about the problem and my/our part in it.
- I/we believe that things must change.
- I/we can see that I/we can be part of the solution.
- I/we have choices to make.
- I/we can see the first steps to change.

Such a framework gives some opportunity for self-assessment by the parent and creates the potential for looking at change.

The quality of the whole child protection assessment and multi-agency approach should be underpinned by the following principles, as outlined in *Framework for the Assessment of Children in Need and their Families* (DoH 2000).

Assessments should:

- be child-centred
- be rooted in child development
- be ecological in approach
- ensure equality of opportunity
- involve working with children and their families
- build on strengths as well as identify weaknesses
- be inter-agency in approach to assessment and provision of services
- be a continuing process, not a one-off event
- be carried out in parallel with other action and also provide services
- be grounded in evidence-based knowledge.

In order to achieve these principles an interactive approach has been developed that brings together three key aspects: the developmental needs of children, the capacities of parents to respond appropriately to those needs, and the impact of wider family and environmental factors on parenting capacity and children. These three interrelated systems have also been called domains and each has a number of critical dimensions.

Dimensions of a child's developmental needs include health, education, emotional and behavioural development, identity, family and social relationships, social presentation and self-care skills. The vitally important role of the teacher is in his or her knowledge of the child in particular and child development in general. The second domain is dimensions of parenting capacity. This includes basic care, ensuring safety, emotional warmth, stimulation, guidance and boundaries, and stability. Thirdly, family and environmental factors consist of family history and functioning, wider family, housing, employment, income, family's social integration and community resources.

Throughout this process the strengths of parents should be identified as well as the difficulties. All this information is crucial in assessing the risk to the child, the potential for change in the parent, the systems around the family and evaluating any planned coherent programme of intervention.

While always maintaining a clear focus on the safety and well-being of the child, the following principles are helpful when planning work with parents. These 15 points are described in *Working Together to Safeguard Children* (DoH 1999) and will apply to teachers within the multi-disciplinary framework.

1. Treat all family members with dignity and respect.
2. Ensure that family members know that the child's safety and welfare must come first, but that each has a right to a courteous, caring and

professionally competent service.

3. Take care not to infringe privacy any more than is necessary to safe-guard the welfare of the child.

4. Be clear with yourself and family members of your powers and duties to intervene and the purpose of your professional involvement at each stage.

5. Be aware of the effects on family members of the power you have as a professional and the impact and implications of what you say and do.

6. Respect the confidentiality of family observations and your observations of them, unless they give you permission to pass on the information to others or it is essential to do so to protect the child.

7. Listen to the concerns of children and their families and take care to learn about their understanding, fears and wishes before arriving at your own explanations and plans.

8. Learn about and consider children within their family relationships and communities, including their religious and cultural contexts, and their place within their own family.

9. Consider the strengths and potential of family members, as well as their weaknesses, problems and limitations.

10. Ensure children, families and other carers know their responsibilities and rights, including any rights to services and their right to refuse services and any consequences of doing so.

11. Use plain, jargon-free language appropriate to the age and culture of each person. Explain unavoidable technical and professional terms.

12. Be open and honest about your concerns and responsibilities, plans and limitations, without being defensive.

13. Allow children and families time to take in and understand concerns and processes. A balance needs to be found between appropriate speed and the needs of people who may need extra time to communicate.

14. Take care to distinguish between personal feelings, values, prejudices and beliefs, and professional roles and responsibilities. Ensure that you have good supervision to check that you are doing so.

15. If a mistake or misinterpretation has been made, or you are unable to keep to an agreement, provide an explanation. Always acknowledge any distress experienced by adults and children and do all you can to keep it to a minimum.                              (DoH 1999)

## Ways forward

Parenting itself can be complex and challenging, as well a highly reward-ing. As Reder *et al.* state (1993):

> A general principle of good-enough parenting is that it requires appro-priate demonstrations of 'care and control', as well as an adequate balance between the two . . . The child must be wanted and treated as a person in his/her own right, whose feelings are respected and of concern to the parent.

These factors also apply to some extent to the parent themselves where their own needs and feelings have to be taken into account. In the same way that, over time, we have found it unhelpful to locate difficulty 'within the child', it is now time to think more of an interactive, systemic model of family and parental functioning and relationships, rather than locating difficulty solely as being 'within the parent'. It may be more helpful and realistic to think about what makes some parents and families vulnerable to harming their children and what can be done to prevent this or stop it from happening again.

It has been shown how vitally important education staff are in the whole of the process of protecting children and working with parents. However, there are some key requirements that need to be developed further and built into the planning and management of schools to enable staff to work most effectively:

- All staff should have access to and should participate in regular, high quality training regarding issues to do with protecting children and working with parents.
- Staff in schools need regular opportunities for good quality consulta-tion with outside professionals, such as educational psychologists, regarding their worries, questions and concerns about any aspect of child protection and working with parents. This should include time and space to think about and reflect on their own practice and how to improve it, as well as feelings generated by such complex and demanding work.
- Opportunities for training and developing work with other core agen-cies such as social services and health should be developed. Child protection work should always be carried out within a multi-agency framework, where each agency's roles and responsibilities are under-stood and where different professional backgrounds complement each other.

- The valuable child development component that all teachers have in their initial training should be enhanced and aspects of parental functioning and family systems added to this knowledge base. There should be an emphasis on using evidence-based practice.
- There is still a great deal to be developed in terms of support programmes and groups etc. for parents about parenting. There are very encouraging signs in this area such as the development in the UK of programmes such as Surestart, early parenting support etc. The focus and location of the school may be a useful one to explore further, particularly as it may help some parents to feel less anxious about school and what it represents for them. The value of other parents sharing what they find difficult and what has helped them is a major factor in the success of such groups.
- A wider child safety, child protection message would help all in the community to be aware that safeguarding children is a community imperative. The other side to this is that supporting parents, particularly those in need, is also a community issue.
- In trying to develop a more emotionally literate or emotionally intelligent society, perhaps we still have a lot to do to get across the notion that it is not the negative feelings we have that are the major problem, it is what we do about them.
- We need to acknowledge the fact that all parents have themselves been children and that many children will become the parents of the future. This creates an opportunity for creative and constructive input addressing the needs of the future generation of parents.

## Summary

Those working with parents who have harmed their children need to be open to finding better ways of understanding and feel supported in carrying out best practice. Through sensitive intervention, many previously abusing parents may come to see themselves and be seen, not as parents who harm their own children, but as parents who can define themselves and their behaviour as caring for their children. We need to care for the parents themselves and support their own development to help achieve this in the interests of the child.

# References

Anonymous (1993) *Guide to the United Nations Convention: The rights of the child*. London: Department of Health Children's Rights Development Unit.

Buchanan, A. (1996) *Cycles of Child Maltreatment: Facts, fallacies and intervention*. Chichester: Wiley.

Calder, M. C. and Horwath, J. (eds) (1999) *Working for Children on the Child Protection Register*. Aldershot: Ashgate Publishing.

Cleaver, H. *et al*. (1999) *Children's Needs: Parenting Capacity. The impact of parental mental illness, problem alcohol and drug use and domestic violence in children's development*. London: The Stationery Office.

Dent, R. (ed.) (1998) *Dangerous Care: Working to protect children*. London: Bridge Child Care.

Department of Health (DoH) (1989) The Children Act. London: HMSO.

Department of Health (DoH) (1999) *Working Together to Safeguard Children*. London: The Stationery Office.

Department of Health (DoH) (2000) *Framework for the Assessment of Children in Need and their Families*. London: The Stationery Office.

Hallgarten, J. (2000) *Parents Exist, OK? Issues and vision for parent–school relationships*. London: Institute for Public Policy Research.

Harskamp, A. (1996) 'Working together to protect children from abuse and neglect', in Sigston, A. *et al*. (1996) *Psychology in Practice with Young People, Families and Schools*, 115–30. London: David Fulton Publishers.

Reder, P. and Duncan, S. (1999) *Lost Innocents: A follow-up study of fatal child abuse*. London: Routledge.

Reder, P. *et al*. (1993) *Beyond Blame: Child abuse tragedies revisited*. London: Routledge.

Sampson, A. and Shepherd, J. (1996) *Newham ACPC: Don't shake the baby campaign*. London: Centre for Institutional Studies, University of East London.

Trowell, J. *et al*. (1996) 'Child sexual abuse: can we beat it? Training perspectives in the educational context', in Jennings, C. and Kennedy, E. (eds) (1996) *The Reflective Professional in Education*, 161–93. London: Jessica Kingsley.

CHAPTER 8

# Working with Carers of Children in Public Care

*Jean Law*

Repeated changes of school and of placement are damaging, not only because of the disruption they cause, but because each change represents an ending. Some young people experience unwanted family breakdown and go on to experience the termination of placements which they do not want to end. Some find it difficult to relate to new carers and trust them, and their carers do not obtain the support they need in time to prevent another crisis and eventual breakdown.

(DfEE 2000)

## Introduction

The focus of this chapter is on children and young people in public care and on issues that exist within their care and education settings. The guidance and recommendations in other chapters on working in partnership with parents/carers will also apply to professionals working with the carers of children in public care. Further specific issues are addressed here.

The chapter has a strong emphasis on children's needs. It is hoped that through the exploration of some of the issues in care and education settings readers will develop a greater understanding of some of the experiences and difficulties that face children and young people and will be more able to support their needs appropriately, including liaison with their carers.

The focus on the needs of children who are in public care has had increasing importance, in both the UK and internationally. There has been increasing tension between the nature and timing of state intervention, the quality of state childcare, the rights of children and parents, and the need to protect children from abuse. These issues have informed debate internationally. Perhaps more powerfully in the UK recently, children in public care have been clearly identified as a distinctive and severely disadvantaged group in the government's highlighted 'social inclusion' initiative.

Over time there have been changes in the terms applied to public care. The phrase 'in care' was used in Britain for many years and was seen to have a stigmatising effect, though, in general, it is still commonly used. The Children Act 1989 (Department of Health (DoH) 1989) introduced new terminology of 'looked after children' intended to imply less permanent and a more shared responsibility of care. The 2000 'Guidance' favoured 'children and young people in public care' (DfEE 2000). State care or public care seem to be phrases that are unambiguous and apply to most countries, and these terms will continue to be used here.

## Historical contexts

Any understanding of the complexities to the public care of children has to be seen against the background of changing paradigms in the nature of childhood and child rearing. For centuries there has been a population of impoverished, orphaned and/or abandoned children. Philanthropic Victorian societies like Dr Barnardo's made provision for such children in vast institutions or sent them overseas as emigrants to seek a 'fresh start' (Redding 1989). The increased use of boarding schools and children 'farmed' out to child minders came with the attendant evils of child abuse and child labour explored in some of Dickens' novels. By the end of the nineteenth century there was a growing awareness of children's rights, including the right to education, and after the First World War an increased interest in the effects of unsettled and abusive backgrounds. Psychological approaches promoted a shift from the concept of 'depraved' children to that of 'deprived' children. The period following the Second World War saw the consolidation of modern concepts about childhood, the development of the welfare state in the UK and the influential 1948 Children Act, which was based largely on the effect of adversity evidenced in the lives of child evacuees (Hayden *et al.* 1999). The rise of the 'teenager', increased delinquency and juvenile crime in the 1950s focused interest on preventative approaches and intervention with an increasing emphasis on the effects of social deprivation rather than psychological factors.

The last 40 years in Britain have seen shifts back and forth in legislation and practices in the care of young people. In the 1960s increased powers of the state to intervene with families, together with the rise of the 'Care Order' as an alternative to punitive sentencing, led to an enormous increase in the numbers of children in public care. Enquiries in the 1980s into the deaths and serious abuse of young children in the care of birth and step-parents and the subsequent focus on child protection led again to more children on child protection registers and entering care. In the late

1980s over 121 children in Cleveland were taken into care following child abuse investigations. Criticism was made of what was seen to be over-zealous disruption to many families and controversial paediatric techniques in investigating abuse. This sharpened the dilemmas that influence contemporary thinking. On one side, current childcare principles have increasingly emphasised the importance of family ties and the need for parents and professionals to work in partnership, and on the other, increased awareness of child abuse or maltreatment has highlighted the risks of family placements to children.

The three main foci of current debate are:

- the tensions that exist between different advantages and disadvantages of family or institutional care
- the powers that the state should hold and how these are best exercised
- the tension between care and control that links childhood deprivation, poverty, delinquency and juvenile crime.


## Contemporary perspectives

The 1989 Children Act (DoH 1989) sought to bring together guidance from existing best practice. It emphasises parental responsibility and support for children and families in partnership with social services and is the foundation of current practice in the UK (Vernon and Sinclair 1998). It should also be seen in the context of the Human Rights Act 1989, which set the European Convention on Human Rights into UK domestic law. It identifies three key principles:

- the welfare of the child is of primary importance
- there should be minimal delay in any interventions
- intervention is only justified if it is better than the alternative (Hayden *et al.* 1999).

The Children Act increased parental rights and responsibilities and also children's rights. In particular children's views were to be actively sought and taken account of. It also increased the state's power to intervene on the basis of 'likely' significant harm and paved the way for a much tighter framework of responsibilities for local authorities. Further legislation and guidance was produced to improve practice in care provision and children's access to education. Both are firmly placed in the Labour Government's initiative to promote social inclusion for disadvantaged groups in society.

The *Quality Protects* (DoH 1998) initiative was aimed at further improving services to families and children in need through a three-year programme for local authority development. The guidance expands the existing notion of the 'duty of care' to 'corporate parenting' of children in public care and gives direct responsibility to local government councillors. It introduced a programme of targets set for local authorities that included development of the knowledge held about children in public care, the improvement of provision through a programme of inspection and the reorganisation and expansion of provision. Most significantly it set in place structures to promote inter-departmental professional joint work. This is important for children in public care because it puts greater emphasis on social services, health and education departments working together to action the long-term plans identified in a child's 'Care Plan'. In 2000 the Department for Education and Employment (DfEE) issued the *Guidance on the Education of Children and Young People in Public Care*. This guidance sought to address the social exclusion experienced by people who had been through public care systems, through recognition that education was the key to change existing identified and familiar patterns of disaffection, drug abuse, unemployment and crime.

## The variety of arrangements for the care of children

In Britain now, as in most countries, children come into the care of the state either on a compulsory basis through the courts or via parental agreement or request. International comparisons show considerable variation in the use of different types of provision and in what is included as part of state care. This can either include or exclude boarding school placements, placements for young offenders, and child and adolescent psychiatric units (Hill 2000). The majority of children are placed in local authority residential homes, fostered with a family, or in private or voluntary facilities.

Large impersonal institutions, children's villages and residential nurseries have now disappeared in the UK. The majority of residential homes do not have education on the premises and in cases of children with emotional and behavioural difficulties (EBD), mental health problems or severe disabilities, placement in a residential special school or specialist treatment centre sometimes takes over from residential home or foster care. In most Western countries residential care establishments are now separated into children's homes and adolescent units geared towards the transition into adult life, with some form of secure accommodation for exceptionally challenging young people.

In Eastern Europe, the use of large institutions differentiated by age and

**Table 8.1** Children in public care in 1985 and in 1995, England (from Berridge and Brodie 1998)

| Placement | 1985 | 1995 |
|---|---|---|
| Foster carers | 35,000 | 31,000 |
| Residential home | 15,000 | 8,000 |
| Birth parents | 12,000 | 3,000 |
| Other | 5,000 | 5,000 |

ability was the subject of media attention during the decline of the communist states. Again, internationally there is a wide variation in the skills and training of staff working in residential homes. For example, North America and Germany have a high number of specialist staff, whereas in the UK, Ireland, Italy and France most residential care staff have no formal qualifications, though they do have access to in-service training (Hill 2000). It follows that there will be varying levels of understanding among staff about different ways of understanding and managing behavioural issues and different priorities given to the needs of children, including education.

Overall, in Western Europe there has been a significant drop in the numbers of children in public care since the 1980s (Madge 1994). In the UK, residential home placement is now overwhelmingly outnumbered by foster care placement, as shown in Table 8.1. In most countries where residential home placement has similarly diminished, overall numbers of children in state care has gone down, with foster care placement remaining steady. In countries where residential care is the most common placement, overall numbers have remained steady or increased. In the USA the number of children in state care overall has increased, partly in relation to drug and crime problems in urban areas (Hill 2000).

## Multiple placements as a feature of children's lives

The majority of children come into public care from families that have experienced hardship, upheaval and breakdown. Many of the children will have been affected by distressing and damaging experiences including abuse and neglect. Some are in public care because of the death or illness of parents, marital difficulties or other circumstances in which their family are (temporarily) unable to care appropriately for them. In the UK currently, less than 2% are in public care because of offences they have committed (DfEE 2000). Bebbington and Miles (1989) compared reasons for children entering public care in 1962 and 1987. They found a decrease of 56% due to parent death or illness, an increase of 15% due to the children's

own emotional and behavioural difficulties and that, overall, a greater proportion were associated with deprived families or had been neglected or
abused.

Whatever the reasons for children being in public care, the impact on
their lives is now recognised to be profound. According to the work of
Bowlby (1998), developmental psychology and attachment theory indicate
that a person's resilience or vulnerability is determined to a very significant degree by the pattern of attachment developed during the early years.
Satisfactory attachment, even to an abusive parent or a loving foster carer,
can result in the capacity to be resilient to stressful situations later in life.
Unsatisfactory attachment, for example, to an inconsistent and unloving
parent or through multiple placements in early life, can have an impact on
how the child will adapt to future carers.

While there is very little published on children's experience of 'coming
into care' there is plenty of anecdotal material and analysis of likely effects.
Children are placed in the position of dealing with extensive loss and separation, from parent/carers, siblings, friends and familiar environments.
They are placed, mostly at short notice, in totally new circumstances for
living and often for their education. Children in Britain now come into
public care very often as some form of crisis intervention and are subject
to short-term 'holding' placements. *Quality Protects* (DoH 1998) highlighted the difficulties created by a lack of choice with regard to placements. The result is that children experience a number of short-term
placements or medium-term stays in placements not considered to be
appropriate but for which there is no alternative. This is particularly true
of children from minority ethnic backgrounds who experience placement
in different cultural settings from their own family. Placement changes are
also frequently the outcome of a breakdown in relationships and may
often be the cause of distress to the looked after child and the foster family.
While foster placement is the desired provision for the large majority of
children, difficulties in finding and sustaining appropriate placements
often means that many children have some experience of a residential
home as part of their placement history. Many children experience a large
number of different placements over the years. There is a clear relationship between schooling difficulties and placement breakdown and either
may precipitate the other. It is the cycle of placement breakdowns and
changes of school, or periods out of school, that lead to disaffected young
people with low self-esteem who become young adults with disadvantaged and socially excluded life-styles.

## Issues in working with parents and carers of children in public care

This next section considers how some of the broader issues identified in relation to children in public care affect the care settings themselves. Children who come into care are now more likely to come from dysfunctional, deprived and/or abusive families. They more frequently present emotional and behavioural difficulties in a way that is enmeshed in their own and their families' history and circumstances. Some of the problems that face the parents of children in care when grappling with the education system also apply to foster carers and care workers. They may not feel blamed in the same way for a child's behaviour but they are likely to experience lack of power in the school situation and may be expected to take on the entire responsibility. This is likely to exacerbate the chance of placement breakdown, especially when the child is not in full-time schooling.

Before exploring these themes in more detail a word of caution is needed. To say that all children in the care system present emotional and behavioural difficulties and that all carers face major problems with education would be both misleading and reinforce stereotypical images that are unhelpful. The difficulties described in this chapter, however, sadly do apply to a large number of children in public care. The majority of children who come into the care system are essentially transient. Their first experience is often a short-term placement during a period of crisis in their family. It is not uncommon for children to experience several such crises and periods of short-term care. Children rarely move straight into a long-term care placement as the current climate continues to favour a return to the birth parents and family as much as possible. Only when this is deemed inappropriate do children go into long-term placements that may include adoption. There are many examples of children living happy and successful lives with new families, and of children overcoming the adverse experiences and circumstances from their past when reunited with their own family. In some cases the stigma attached by some to being 'in care' can hinder this process.

## Issues for birth parents and families

It is important to remember that children very rarely come into public care unknown to professionals. The variety and severity of family problems such as poor housing, illness or death, mental health problems, poverty, crime, neglect, abuse and drug use may have featured in the family history and whole families or individual members may have been the focus of professional intervention in the past. Not all such interventions lead to dissatisfaction and failure, but in the current climate when a child is placed in public care it inevitably means that things have gone wrong somewhere. The family are unable to care for the child, or are deemed to be inappropriate carers.

In many cases the move into public care is the result of a breakdown in the relationship between parent and child, possibly as an outcome of the perceived difficult behaviour of the child (Bebbington and Miles 1989). Family breakdown and reconfiguration are familiar features of Western society today, and the stresses that arise are well known. Many parents and children come through such traumas and continue effectively as single parent families or with new groupings providing step-parents and step-siblings. Many parents and children, however, do not make these transitions effectively. The presence of a step-family, loss and separation from a parent and possibly friends and school, possible overcrowded housing conditions and often poverty may all have their impact on how the child copes. In such circumstances it is not uncommon for children to express their feelings through acting out and oppositional behaviour, or for parents to use 'going into care' as a threat in the hope of bringing children into line. The dynamics of family systems and coping mechanisms are complex, but at times of stress children are sometimes identified and 'scape-goated' as the cause of all that has gone wrong.

In Britain children currently coming into public care are more likely to be teenagers (Berridge and Brodie 1998). In these circumstances parents may feel a strong sense of relief when the young person is away, if only in respite care. In facing the inevitable sense of failure that follows from a child going into public care, parents are likely to feel a range of strong emotions, including anger, rejection and guilt. Professionals, including teachers, working with children and parents in these circumstances need to demonstrate extraordinary care, tact and non-judgemental approaches. This can be more than usually difficult when the same professionals are involved in child protection procedures following disclosure from a child.

Current legislation and guidance in the UK provide a framework for shared care where the parent and local authority social services department have shared parental responsibility. Where a return home is initially seen as the way forward, plans will be made to bring this about. Social services staff and other professionals need to adopt approaches that will support and engage parents, where their views and feelings, as well as those of the child, are taken into account. Over time it sometimes becomes apparent that the adults concerned are not able to offer useful and effective parenting. Sadly, parents who love and want to have their children back may offer unrealistic promises and leave the child with false hopes. For many children with a long history of time in care or in long-term placements, occasional contact or loss of contact with parents, siblings and other family members is a very common experience. Children who perceive themselves as rejected can be very difficult to manage at school. They will try their best to 'get in first' and do the rejecting or behave in such a way that teachers fulfil their expectations of rejection. Schools who make a great effort to accept the child (while not condoning their behaviour) may be giving that student a rare positive experience in their relationships with others.

## Foster placement issues

The majority of foster placements in the UK currently are short-term placements. The shortage of foster carers and the difficulties of finding appropriate placements often mean that children are placed for longer periods than planned in a given foster family. The placement may only be considered inappropriate for the longer term because of issues like the distance to the birth family or from school, or in relation to other foster children currently living with the family. Close mutual attachments are sometimes formed causing distress to both parties when the placement ends. Foster carers can face challenges of linking with birth families or adoptive families when a child they have cared for and are fond of moves from their home.

A number of factors lead to the breakdown of foster placements where the carers find the child challenging and request that they be moved. One frequent strain that is put on foster placements is where the child is not attending school regularly. Rivalry and failure to get along with other foster children in the home or the birth children of the foster carers are also common causes, as is the child's lack of cooperation with family and home rules, for example, in keeping bedrooms tidy and times for coming home. In themselves these issues may be no more serious than are the ordinary disputes between parents and children, but they take on a different perspective when negotiations are taking place between people who may have only known each other a short while, and where there is no mutual obligation or expectancy of permanence.

Nissim (1997) has suggested a number of factors which research into the effectiveness of long-term placements indicates lead to success. These include:

- the maintenance of satisfactory contact with birth parents and siblings
- birth parents' continued involvement with local authority staff in planning for their child
- the child's acceptance and understanding of why they are in public care
- the child's motivation to make the placement work
- foster parents' experience, preparation, training and support
- the age and attitudes of the foster family's children
- the active and sensitive involvement of social workers.

*Quality Protects* initiatives have increased the training and support for foster carers and a move to more professionalism, especially for hard-to-place young people. One way that schools can support foster carers is by focusing on providing a welcoming positive school experience for the young person which may help to improve their attendance. Where positive actions are also jointly planned in school for a child, then this will perhaps give guidance and ideas to foster carers who may otherwise be struggling in their role. Validation of the child's feelings and modelling listening skills are just two ways in which schools can take a lead role. There can be as much collusion about acceptance and pro-active planning as there can about a focus on difficulties and labelling.

## Residential placement issues

Compared with trends in the mid-1980s, few children now stay in residential homes for lengthy periods, though even those who are intended to have short-term placement may be unable to return home so that their stay extends for months or years (Chakrabarti and Hill 2000). For the most part, residential placement is seen as something to be avoided except as a last resort, though for a few children for whom family placement has proved to be inappropriate, residential homes are the preferred or only option. The majority of children placed are over 12 years of age, and many residential homes run special programmes for care leavers. Many young people move on to more specialist provision for the transition into adult life. In the UK children can still be removed from public care at 16 years of age, but there are increased responsibilities and provision in local authorities for support and supervision up to 18 years.

Most residential homes now are small, purpose built establishments that are intended to fit into the local neighbourhood. In Britain, as in some other countries, low pay, unsociable hours and stressful work conditions result in a high turnover of staff (Berridge and Brodie 1998). Frequent changes of staff, together with regular movement of children, can create a climate of impermanence in many homes. Care workers usually work shift patterns, with staff taking turns to sleep over each night. Most homes operate a 'key worker' system where one person is assigned to be the principle carer for a child and to be the link person with the child's parents, social worker, school etc. The shift working has an impact on the availability of key workers to communicate with school or to help with homework. It is, however, useful for schools to identify a child's key worker, give them good notice of important meetings and be flexible in home–school liaison so that there is as much consistency of communication as possible.

## Implications for education

School can provide the one source of continuity and stability in an otherwise turbulent and uncertain life. When consulted, children in care say that they like school and want to be there. Some describe it as a lifeline. As well as a place to acquire skills and knowledge, school is somewhere to make friends and learn about relationships, and to receive praise and encouragement.                                                    (DfEE 2000)

### The role of education in the life of children in public care

The educational needs of children in public care have been seen as of limited importance compared with the imperatives of identifying and maintaining a safe care environment and continuity of contact with natural family members where possible. Local authorities in Britain have not routinely collected information on the educational status and attainment of children in public care. However, shocking data on their low educational attainment and life outcomes have gradually emerged through a variety of research and reports. Vernon and Sinclair (1998) found that in 1998:

- 20% were not on any school roll
- 75% of young people in public care would leave school with no qualifications at all, compared with 6% nationally
- 3% would have five public examination passes compared to 64% nationally
- 80% of ex-care people aged 18 to 24 were unemployed
- 61% of prisoners under 21 had been in public care.

It was these kinds of statistics that identified children in care as underachieving, disadvantaged and socially excluded.

Many children in public care are identified as showing challenging behaviour, to have some special educational needs and to be subject to exclusion from school. Children in public care have been up to ten times more likely to be excluded from school compared with children in general. In addition, there is informal exclusion through non-admission or failure to pursue non-attendance. In 1995 60 per cent of children living in residential homes were reported to be non-school attenders (DoH OFSTED 1995). The pre-care life experiences of children in public care, as well as broken schooling, stigmatisation and poor continuity of care, have been identified as factors in children's low educational attainment, disaffection, non-attendance and exclusion from school. Other research has suggested that by the time the question of care arises many children's educational problems have been identified, and themselves contribute to the decision to place the child in public care.

There has been a tendency to treat children in public care as a homogeneous group, without regard to individual or group differences, for example, those who are disabled as well as in public care and those from minority ethnic groups. Jackson (1995) identified shared characteristics of a group of 'successful' care leavers (with careers and experience of higher education). Continuity of schooling during periods of being in care was seen to be the most crucial factor in their success, as well as early reading opportunities and contact with birth parents who showed an interest in education.

The messages from children and young people themselves, reflected in the quotation above from *Guidance on the Education of Children and Young People in Public Care* (DfEE 2000), have been clear and consistent. They also say that they often feel excluded from normal activities and opportunities and are assumed to be troublesome. They report that in school they are subject to bullying, name-calling and intrusive questioning. It is clear that many find it too difficult to maintain their education in the face of the range of obstacles and difficulties to overcome.

## Suggestions for school action

The 2000 Guidance (DfEE 2000) was introduced to promote 'corporate parenting' and joint action at local authority level, affecting education, social services and health departments as well as outlining the responsibilities of schools. The guidance required local authorities to ensure that:

- each child in care had a personal education plan
- educational needs should be satisfactorily arranged as an element of all placements except in emergencies

- no child should be without an education placement for more than 20 days
- there should be local systems for the collection and sharing of relevant data about children in public care.

The guidance also introduced the role of 'designated teacher' for children in public care who would act as an advocate for the young person, as the link with multi-agency workers and help provide the young person with access to support and services needed. The teacher should coordinate information about past educational history and future needs, and take responsibility for the personal education plan. The personal education plan should incorporate a record of the pupil's achievement, developmental and educational needs, short-term targets and long-term plans. The plan should form part of the overall Care Plan and be reviewed with it, every six months.

Many children in public care have presented considerable problems to their schools. Meeting their complex needs can be time consuming and may seem to have limited effect. Many dedicated and caring teachers may themselves feel helpless in their capacity to make a difference for children who already have a range of professional workers. Children and young people who are themselves under tremendous strain, suffering from loss, anger and disorientation, may not be the easiest or most cooperative people. Where they present aggressive and oppositional behaviour it can affect other children as much as it does teachers and the learning environment.

Identified good practice and research have suggested that schools can develop policies and practices that support, and do not disadvantage, the young person in public care who may be a long-term pupil of the school experiencing period(s) of difficulty, or a transient or short-term member experiencing changes of placement. Such approaches include:

- an inclusive admissions policy
- seeking to minimise the use of exclusion of children in public care
- the development of staff skills and systems to support the needs of children with emotional and behavioural difficulties and promote the understanding of young people's mental health needs and difficulties
- close links and co-working with education support services and multi-disciplinary work
- any special educational needs should be identified as early as possible and interventions put into place. School leavers need to have support for strong links with careers services and further education opportunities.

Schools are potentially of very great importance to the child in public care: for stability, consistency, acceptance and promoting a sense of achievement. They have been marginalised in the past but are now becoming a more central consideration in planning and provision. Schools need to ensure that relevant staff take an active part in both formal and informal meetings. Establishing a 'key worker' in school for a child in public care also helps to maintain consistency and develop positive relationships. This is important both for the child and for the professional carer. Although a demand on teacher time, it may be more effective than frequent crisis intervention.

There is also a potential issue for working with 'professional carers' which is particularly true of those who have a more transient relationship with the child. Where both school and a carer are having similar experiences and difficulties with a young person there is a danger that they collude in labelling and focusing on the management of behaviour rather than on the needs of the whole child. The child is then left without an advocate. The *in loco parentis* functions mentioned in Chapter 6 need an equal emphasis in order for the child to have an appropriate experience. Conversely a professional and skilled approach from a teacher may provide a model for positive responses and interactions. As with some parents, carers may value the learning that comes with joint planning.

## Summary

While it is true that some people experience time in public care as a positive influence on their lives, for the majority the experience has a very negative and often long-lasting effect. Changing paradigms in the care and provision made for children whose family experience difficulty in caring for them appropriately have resulted in a complex and confusing contemporary context. Birth families, foster carers and residential establishments are all able to provide both good and bad care experiences for children. It is clear that access to education can have a fundamental and sustained impact on the lives of children whose childhood has been disrupted and disjointed. Schools can best help to provide that access by creating an ethos and climate that is inclusive of children in public care but also seeks to promote education positively in their lives. All professionals working with children in public care and with parent/carers need to listen carefully to the views of the children and adults and to act as their advocates.

# References

Bebbington, A. and Miles, J. (1989) 'The background of children who enter local authority care', *British Journal of Social Work* **20**, 283–307.

Berridge, D. and Brodie, I. (1998) *Children's Homes Revisited.* London: Jessica Kingsley.

Bowlby, J. (1998) 'Developmental psychiatry comes of age', *American Journal of Psychiatry* **145**(1), 1–10.

Chakrabarti, M. and Hill, M. (eds) (2000) *Residential Child Care.* London: Jessica Kingsley.

Department for Education and Employment (DfEE) (2000) *Guidance on the Education of Children and Young People in Public Care.* London: HMSO.

Department of Health (DoH) (1989) The Children Act. London: HMSO.

Department of Health (DoH) (1998) *Quality Protects: Transforming children's services.* London: DoH.

Department of Health (DoH), Social Services Inspectorate/OFSTED (1995) *The Education of Children Who Are Looked After By Local Authorities.* London: OFSTED.

Hayden, C. *et al.* (1999) *State Child Care: Looking after children?* London: Jessica Kingsley.

Hill, M. (2000) 'The residential child care context', in Chakrabarti, M. and Hill, M. (eds.) *Residential Child Care.* London: Jessica Kingsley.

Jackson, S. (1995) *Transforming Lives: The crucial role of education for young people in the care system.* London: Who Cares Trust.

Madge, N. (1994) *Children in Residential Care in Europe.* London: National Children's Bureau.

Nissim, R. (1997) 'Children living in substitute families', *Educational and Child Psychology* **14**(2), 4–12.

Redding, D. (1989) 'The little slaves', *Community Care* 4 May, 19–20.

Vernon, J. and Sinclair, R. (1998) *Maintaining Children in School: The contribution of social services departments.* London: National Children's Bureau.

# CHAPTER 9

# Working with Mobile Families

*Anthea Wormington*

Pupil mobility is 'a child joining or leaving a school at a point other than the normal age at which children start or finish their education at that school, whether or not this involves a move of home.'

(Dobson and Henthorne 1999: 5)

## Definition

For the purposes of this chapter highly mobile families are defined as those with children who are in a school for less than a complete term. Families may be mobile, at different times, for various reasons. Their mobility may be due to their life-style or their particular family circumstances at that time.

Mobile families may include Travellers, refugees, asylum seekers, homeless families and children whose parents serve in the armed forces. Sometimes children in public care are mobile as they move from one placement to another (see Chapter 8). The word 'Traveller' is defined for educational purposes as people who either have, or have had in the past, a traditionally nomadic life-style, where they have worked as they have travelled. This will include Romany Gypsy Travellers, Travellers – who sometimes prefer not to be called 'Gypsies' – such as fairground families or show people, circus families, new Travellers, bargees and other families living on boats. The word 'Gypsy' is the proper name of an ethnic group and comes from the proper noun Egyptian. It should be spelt with a capital letter. The word 'Traveller' should also be spelt with a capital letter when it refers to the group of people that includes Gypsies.

A family may find themselves in a situation of high mobility either by choice or through circumstances. It can be caused by social deprivation or family break-up, especially where domestic violence is involved, temporary accommodation, rented housing, families seeking refuge or asylum status and certain types of employment including seasonal work and the armed forces. Although very different in many respects, mobility is a core issue.

## Introduction

The vast majority of mobile children settle into school well, causing little concern to the school but there are specific behavioural issues that may arise due to mobility. Some children may arrive at a new school having witnessed, or been involved in, violent confrontations. They may be agitated or traumatised, needing stability, structure and a sense of calm and reassurance from the school. Having moved around many schools these children may be behind with their education and try to disguise feelings of inadequacy by withdrawing into themselves, refusing to cooperate, or behaving disruptively. If schools are made aware of the possible issues around mobility they may be able to put strategies into place for working with the parents that will benefit not only the child but the school too.

The Dobson Report (Dobson *et al.* 2000), which is the outcome of a government funded study on pupil mobility in England and Wales, found that children with learning and behavioural difficulties were often disproportionately represented among mobile children and this was largely engendered by factors associated with the mobility. Children were often not in one place long enough for their special educational needs to be properly identified and fully assessed, even when they were severe, complex and long term. Others were able children who fell seriously behind their peer group because of disrupted schooling.

## Issues for schools

Mobility presents particular problems because the school system is designed for a static population and children that do not live in one place for any length of time have problems being included within it. These children often lack a sense of belonging and may feel marginalised socially and academically. They may feel lost and uncomfortable in the school environment unless specific programmes are rapidly put into place to promote inclusion. This may result in the child's motivation to attend school disappearing altogether and possibly the parent's desire to get the child to school!

Schools are under constant pressure to improve attendance and achievement targets and the school curriculum assumes that the child will be at school every day and, indeed, remain there. There are difficulties for the child, the teacher and the school if the child misses any part of the curriculum. The education system assumes that a child of a certain age will be at a specific level of experience and attainment at their chronological age and makes little allowance for missed education or lack of previous school experience. The acquisition of school records from previous schools can be a lengthy process and not always possible.

Schools with large numbers of children living in temporary accommodation often experience attendance problems. Temporary accommodation may often be overcrowded and this is not conducive to learning. It may be difficult to sleep with everyone in the same room watching television, babies crying, nowhere to keep books, nowhere quiet to read books or do homework. There may be shared beds and bedrooms, nowhere to keep clothing and the heating might not be very efficient.

Poor attendance and poor punctuality are not viewed favourably and often seen in an unsympathetic light. Schools may, however, be very reluctant to admit mobile children at certain times in the year, for example when annual assessments and examination schedules are underway.

### Families' perceptions

There can be a mismatch between the school's perception of the family's commitment to education and the actual facts. With background knowledge of mobility issues the school may be able to cross this bridge. Without this knowledge, though, the school may think that the parents have no interest in the child's education and use their own value judgements to assess the child's welfare. The school may even be critical of the way it perceives the child is being cared for. The actual reason that parents of mobile children may appear to the school to be unsupportive is because, with everything else that is going on in the lives of the members of the family, education may not be their first priority. Some refugee children may even have witnessed the killing of people close to them.

---

# Case study: Mehmet

Mehmet was a fourteen-year-old boy whose father had been killed. He was now head of the family. His mother was both ill and depressed and he had to look after the younger children. When a teacher told him off for being late for school and not wearing the correct uniform he swore at the teacher and walked out of the school.

---

If the school tries to build strong supportive relationships through out-reach work, liaison with the families and local support networks within the community, this will develop knowledge and sensitivity to the home circumstances of the children.

## Issues for families

If a family is living in a highly populated area they may have to wait many weeks before there is a vacancy for their child in a local school. If the family moves often this could amount to days or weeks of missed school-ing each time they await a school placement. Alternatively they could be offered a place a long way from where they live. Being dependent upon unreliable transport may result in frequent lateness or missing even more days of schooling. The school may be unaware of all this and perceive it as a lack of interest in education. If the family is large they usually wish their children to go to the same school, usually the nearest. There may not be enough spaces available for everyone and if the family has a number of children in different establishments getting them all to school on time may be a near impossibility.

Although times have changed, the parents may themselves not have been to school or have had negative experiences. It is only in the last 20 years that Travellers have been included in mainstream education, in class-rooms being taught alongside other children. Prior to this they were often taught in units, on caravan sites or in separate provision. Before that the majority had no schooling at all. Alternatively mobile children may have been placed at the back of the classroom to do pictures while the rest of the class were taught the full curriculum. Families may view the school with suspicion and expect teachers automatically to take the part of the settled community if there is a dispute of any kind because this is what they are used to. The parents are often overwhelmed when they see the work their children can produce on computers.

## Issues for the child

When the child is placed in yet another school with a lot of new faces he or she may get into trouble for being late, not wearing the correct uniform, not bringing in absence notes and for being unable to produce work of the same quality as the other children. Such children may then see them-selves as a nuisance; they may feel anxious, uneasy and inadequate. They may start withdrawing into themselves, refusing to cooperate or behaving disruptively. They may also feel really unhappy and lonely especially at playtime and lunch-times if they have no friends to play with.

## Initial interview

Many of these problems may be resolved with understanding the situation and building trusting relationships between the school and the families. This can start with the initial interview. Showing understanding and making the child and the family feel welcome in the school is very important. The first person the family meets in the school is usually the school administrator. A warm and friendly approach that reflects the ethos of the school is critical. At the interview it is crucial to have someone who speaks the same language as the family. It is helpful if the school makes it clear that they are willing to make allowances over school uniform. They can make a note of the family's phone number and perhaps suggest the family phone if the child is away or likely to be late.

## Establishing positive relationships

It may be possible to arrange ways where the child will have someone to play with them at playtime and, perhaps, a child to show them around the school. However good the structures and systems are within a school, learning and behaviour have always been dependent upon the relationships between the pupil and individuals within that school. An unhappy student never learns as well as a happy student.

## Addressing practical problems

Families who are mobile because of accommodation problems may be living in temporary or short-stay accommodation. Poverty and poor accommodation often go together. Personal hygiene may be a problem caused by poor facilities within the accommodation. There may be limited washing facilities, for example there may be no washing machine, a shortage of hot water, one bathroom that has to be shared by a very large family. Some schools have arranged for children to have showers at school, kept changes of clothing and when absolutely necessary even washed clothing in a machine in school. Money may be short and this may result in the family not being able to afford school uniform, especially when a different school uniform is needed for each new school the child attends. All of these issues may hinder the child's successful integration into school.

## Illiteracy

Parents may be unable to read and write or reluctant to send their children to school due to their own lack of, or negative, school experiences. This may result in the children's homework not being completed, appropriate forms not returned, unwillingness to send children on school trips and the parent's reluctance to visit school. If the family are newly entered into the country they may not understand English.

## Racism

'Travelling children are likely to be amongst the most educationally disadvantaged unless schools take steps to ensure their inclusion' (OFSTED 1996). Throughout history the static population have always viewed newcomers, and people who move around, with fear and suspicion. Each time a mobile family moves into an area the family are regarded, by the sedentary population, as newcomers.

   Once gaining access to a school Traveller and refugee children in particular may encounter particular problems with racism and stereotyping. This may occur because the school has either not experienced Travellers or refugees or has limited experience of these ethnic groups and their cultures. The school may find itself prejudiced by stereotypical attitudes portrayed, promoted and perpetuated by the press and media. Travellers are either depicted as romantic figures with their wagons, horses, camp-fires, music, dancing and free life-style or more often both they and refugees are reported in an extremely negative light as 'dirty' or 'thieving scroungers'. There has been extensive coverage on asylum-seeking refugees who have, according to the media, run away, or paid to be smuggled, from countries where they are not in danger, to live in other countries where they can receive state handouts for food and housing. These stories are highly damaging to the many families who have fled in fear of their lives and often lost everything in the process. These negative stereotypical attitudes may be passed on to the parents of the children in the school and then to their children. This can result in the Traveller and refugee children experiencing bullying, name-calling and having difficulty making friends within their peer groups.

> # Case study: Travellers
>
> A Traveller encampment was parked opposite a school. The Travellers wanted to send their children to the school and there were places for the 12 children. The parents of children already attending the school threatened to withdraw their children if these Traveller children were admitted. The children were admitted. It was just before Christmas. Parents attended the Christmas Bazaar and all the children were involved in the Christmas parties. By the time the Travellers moved on in January the school and the parents living in the area were sorry to see them go.

## Culture

Traveller and various refugee cultures and life-styles have historically been absent from the school curriculum. Projects on homes for instance have very rarely included trailers or caravans. There has always been an assumption that homes are static.

When Traveller children reach their teens, the Traveller family often views them as adults. The older girls are expected to look after their younger siblings and the boys to go out to work with their fathers. As the children are used to being treated as adults their behaviour towards teachers may be deemed at times to be inappropriate. They may appear to be too familiar in the way they speak to adults and by not realising that they are expected to keep an appropriate physical distance from teachers. Students unaware of the protocol may have to have this explained to them.

Attendance at secondary school is often deemed inappropriate. Traveller boys in their early teens are expected to be out working with their families earning money and learning a trade. They may see anything but reading and writing, especially examinations, as a waste of their time as they have a career already. If they are in school under duress this may adversely affect their behaviour. College placements and work experience can be a solution to this. An example is the fifteen-year-old Traveller boy who was allowed to work part of the week with his father as 'work experience' while he attended school part time. Where secondary education is encouraged the family may want single-sex schools because of their religious and cultural beliefs.

Large dangly earrings are often regarded by some Travellers as something girls wear as part of their culture. Schools are used to dealing with children having to dress specifically because of their culture and religion. Sikh boys are expected to keep their turbans on in school and some

Moslem girls are expected to keep their legs covered at all times even when swimming.

---

## Case study: Traveller girl

A mother of a thirteen-year-old Traveller girl was upset because her daughter was not allowed to wear her earrings in school. The mother was reluctant to come to discuss the problem because she did not feel comfortable in the school. The Traveller Support Officer offered to accompany her to talk with the child's Head of Year. The Head of Year showed the mother around the school and she witnessed a physical education lesson. The danger of wearing earrings in PE was discussed and the safety aspect stressed. The mother agreed that it would be safer for her daughter to have plasters over the earrings during PE and the school allowed the girl to wear the earrings the rest of the time.

---

Many cultures also have a different view of discipline within the school and which behaviours are considered more or less important. Issues related to school regulations for instance may not be seen as a priority.

## Inclusion

Today most schools try to include the great majority of children within their system and there has been a move in the UK and elsewhere for schools to become much more inclusive. The 1981 Education Act (DES 1981) heralded the end of separate provision and saw the way to mainstream classrooms having children with special needs integrated within them. It also began the movement towards the closure of segregated provision and the reorganisation of support. Since the early 1990s there has been a move away from the notion of integration towards inclusion. The word 'integration' has been used to describe processes by which individual children are supported in order that they can participate in the existing (and largely unchanged) programme of the school. 'Inclusion', by contrast, suggests willingness from the school to restructure its programme in response to the diversity of pupils who attend. 'Inclusive education' needs to focus not only on children with special needs related to learning but also children whose needs are due to their social circumstances. Both learning and behaviour may become an issue for these children if not addressed proactively.

Schools have always found it more difficult to include children with behavioural difficulties but the inflexible structure of some schools can accentuate difficult behaviour from certain groups of children. Mobile children may present difficult behaviour that can be overcome if the structure of the school is flexible enough to accommodate them and this does not have to be at the expense of the other children in the school. Indeed, it should benefit the whole school and all the children within it.

## Working together to overcome the problems

The Dobson Report found that all the mobile children in their study needed attention and support (Dobson *et al.* 2000). Most schools are able to use support or advice from outside agencies to help include mobile children. There is a concern, however, that any kind of additional outside resource takes time and effort to obtain. This should not be the case. Many LEAs in Britain have teams with responsibilities for dealing with both refugee and Traveller children. Traveller Education Services (TESs) in particular are used to dealing quickly and flexibly with sudden influxes of children and should have systems in place to cater for this. These teams have valuable expertise when it comes to dealing with particular groups of mobile children. Their skill, good practice and methods of working can often be used with all mobile children.

## Ways of supporting mobile families and examples of good practice

### *Prior to accessing school*

'Whereas with other groups of children . . . we have been chiefly concerned with their needs within schools, many of the particular educational needs of Travellers' children arise because of difficulties in gaining access to the education system at all' (DES 1985). This statement is probably true of most mobile children residing in a densely populated area and additional help may be necessary to access these groups to school. This may be in the form of home visits to the family, telephoning schools and the LEA on behalf of the family and arranging appointments, interpreters, free-dinner forms etc. It may also be necessary to point the family to voluntary sector support groups, or advice groups dealing with housing benefits and accommodation problems. Much work may have been done with the family before they even get to the school.

## Accessing school

The initial visit is important. Schools can be very daunting places with big, locked security gates. Many schools now have parent rooms and posters around the school in many different languages advising families where to go for help and advice on issues such as domestic violence. This shows families that schools are aware of certain issues and they are not alone with their problems.

## Provision of school uniform

School uniform can impede integration, as it often has to be bought from specific shops at a non-discounted price, usually before the pupil starts school. If a child moves frequently the provision of uniform can become very expensive. It does not help the children to feel comfortable in school if they are dressed differently to their peers. Although some LEAs still have clothing grants these are usually available only once a year and are means tested.

It is useful if schools can be aware and have a list of outside agencies that might be able to assist with money for uniform. TESs often have money in their budgets to be used, on a discretionary basis, for uniform. There may be local support groups or churches that can help or a school may have money in its budget for specific cases. Social services may be able to help out in exceptional cases. Some schools keep boxes of second-hand uniform to give out when necessary.

## Once in school

Once the mobile child is in school the type of support offered must depend upon the skills and experience of the pupil. If the child has attended school before, a quick transfer of records from the previous school is important. TESs can often help with getting hold of school records for Traveller children if they know the last area in which they were living.

A mid-phase assessment, as soon as the child is in school, is useful to identify appropriate programmes of academic or social support and, if necessary, the involvement of outside agencies.

## Home visits

Some schools have teachers that have an outreach role within the school. Initially this may be a useful form of support for the family. Home visits help build a trusting relationship between the school and family and if the family are unable to read or write this may be an invaluable way of communicating information. If the child is away and no absence note is forthcoming a visit is also useful. The family can often be encouraged to ring the school if they have a phone. Schools may find it useful to have a special form for parents who do not read and write to complete if their children are ill. This procedure would also be helpful for families who do not speak English. It is often reassuring for the child to see a teacher that they know visiting them at home. This strengthens the relationship between the child and teacher and can have a positive effect on the child's behaviour in school. Often when a child has been absent, a visit to the family, just to let them know that the school has noticed, may result in the child being back at school the next day.

---

## Case study: Absent child

On one occasion a child had not been in school. The support teacher went around to see the family. She sat in their lounge and asked if the child was well. The mother said that he had been absent because he had come out in a rash because he was allergic to the iguana and so had had to go and stay with his aunt. The teacher was asked if she wanted to see the iguana. The teacher expressed an interest and was told to get up because the iguana was behind her seat. Sure enough there was a three-legged iguana about 2 feet long! It had lost a leg in a fight with its brother in the cage at the pet shop. The child was back at school the next day. The story had probably been the first story the mother could think of being caught 'on the hop' but that did not matter. The aim of the visit had been achieved.

---

### Mobile phones

Mobile phones have been a great invention for mobile families. Many have these rather than land phones if they are moving around a lot. They also have uses when maintaining discipline in the school. This needs to be with the prior agreement of the parent and with their understanding of how such a measure fits in with a positive behaviour policy. It is useful for the child to know that there are links between home and school and active contact with the family.

---

# Case study: Use of mobile phone

A child had been behaving badly in the classroom with a supply teacher covering the class for the day. Some mobile children may respond badly to changes within their classroom, as they feel secure with set routines. The support teacher took the child out of the classroom and in front of him phoned his father on his mobile phone. His father asked to speak to the boy and afterwards he was well behaved for the rest of the day.

On another occasion a seven-year-old girl was being particularly stubborn with the teacher at carpet time. Already that day she had been caught bullying another child in the class. The teacher phoned her mother there and then. The mother asked to talk to her daughter and as a result the girl apologised to the girl she had been unkind to and behaved for the rest of the day.

---

## Social skills

Children with no previous schooling may need support in acquiring the social skills necessary to survive in the classroom. Initially it may be helpful for someone to work with them and also to familiarise them with the classroom rules. This may mean working within a group of children in the class helping the child socialise and cooperate with other children.

One school made a point of employing a Traveller classroom assistant. There were quite a few Travellers on the roll and the behaviour of a minority had been causing concern. The assistant's role was to work with various groups of children, not solely the Traveller children. She was a very positive role model for the Traveller children within that school and this helped to build a more positive and trusting relationship between the school and the Traveller families. They became much more confident in approaching the school.

Another method of support could be the employment of a 'buddy system'. This is where children within the class are given the job of 'befriending' a new child, showing them where to go and what to do within the school.

## Curriculum input

Differentiation of the curriculum is another way in which support may be offered. Schools may choose to use outside teams to help plan and deliver back-up schemes of work as well as the routine differentiation that the class teacher organises.

Difficulties often occur when a school organises and delivers its curriculum without responding to all its pupils as individuals. Many schools introduce additional materials into the school's curriculum that are relevant to mobile families. They either choose to buy these or borrow them from resource bases.

When a family was studying homes a Traveller grandfather once came and showed the children a caravan that he had made. He explained how he'd made it and how the living area inside the caravan was used. The same man had a plot of land with horses and chickens on it and he used to invite the classes from the school to visit the plot for project work or art classes.

A varied curriculum, and different teaching styles, can positively influence the motivation of children in the classroom and thus increase their learning. Theatre groups often deal with social issues in interesting ways. Partnership teaching with a specialist or support teacher can also be a useful resource.

---

## Case study: Breaking down barriers

There were a lot of Asian children in the class and one Traveller girl. The Traveller girl's behaviour had been a cause for concern and her relationships with the other children had been causing problems; there had been name-calling on both sides. The lesson pointed out that Romany Gypsies had most probably come from India. The Asian girls were very interested in this and became much more accepting of the Traveller afterwards. There was a fashion show at the end of term, which gave the Traveller girl an excuse to wear a sari. It didn't seem to matter that she was in fact an Irish Traveller and her roots probably not Indian at all!

---

### Lack of literacy

Many teaching methods can rely to a great extent on reading and writing activities, and may present a problem to a mobile pupil whose literacy skills are behind that of their peer group. All pupils need to learn to read and write and this is what families expect to get from school. Unless these skills are learnt at an early stage it makes it very difficult for the child to function at later stages in the curriculum. With inclusive education some schools have begun to take the stance that any withdrawal from the classroom is taboo. There are, however, occasions when it might be appropriate for the child to be withdrawn from the classroom, either by themselves or with a group of other children, for a 'catch-up' programme in basic literacy. The educational needs of the individual child are paramount. All such programmes should be explained to parents so they know what is on offer for their child. Schools also need to maintain awareness of the literacy levels of families and not make assumptions about skills they may or may not have, which will vary greatly from one family to another.

## Outings

Families may be reluctant to send their children on school trips and outings. They may be unhappy about entrusting their child to the school and/or be worried about the cost. Whether or not a child goes on an outing may well be a measure of how included they feel within the school. This trust has to be built gradually.

---

### Case study: School trip

A class were going on a trip to a farm. A mother was reluctant to allow her child on the trip. The child could be disruptive and the school were concerned that he would not behave. His mother was not happy about the coach trip but the school needed extra adults and so this parent was asked to come. She accepted and the child went also.

---

## Homework

An inclusive school is one that is accepting of all children, but each school does have great pressure on it to perform well and achieve a good level of attainment. This may mean that success in the classroom is dependent, to a large extent, on homework being completed in the child's own time. Mobile children may find this problematic because of conditions at home. They may have no space in which to do school work or keep their things, and there may be many small children running around. Their parents may be unable to read and write and not be able to give the necessary help and support. A way some schools avoid this problem is by running homework clubs in school either at lunchtimes or after school.

## Summary

Most schools realise that mobile children are the responsibility of the school as much as any other child. This means developing strategies and policies to incorporate these children into the everyday routines, ensure that they have access to the curriculum and find ways to help them feel part of the school community. Good liaison with families facilitates this process.

The aims of any service involved with mobile children should be, not just to support the individual child and family, but also to bring the families, children and schools closer together. Where the curriculum, policies and pastoral systems are in place so that mobile children are included within them, external support can be targeted most appropriately to support the school.

## References

Ainscow, M. (1998) 'Exploring links between special needs and school improvement', *Support for Learning* **13**(2), 70–5. Nasen.

Bastiani, J. (ed.) (1997) *Home–School Work in Multicultural Settings*. London: David Fulton Publishers.

Department of Education and Science (DES) (1981) The Education Act. London: HMSO.

Department of Education and Science (DES) (1985) *Education for All: The report of the Committee of Inquiry into the Education of Children from Ethnic Minority Groups*. Chairman Lord Swann. London: The Stationery Office.

Dobson, J. and Henthorne, K. (1999) *Pupil Mobility in Schools: Interim report*. London: The Stationery Office.

Dobson, J. *et al.* (2000) *Pupil Mobility in Schools: Final report*. London: University College London.

Gray, J. and Richer, J. (1991) *Classroom Responses to Disruptive Behaviour*. London: Routledge.

Kiddle, C. (1999) *Traveller Children: A voice for themselves*. London: Jessica Kingsley.

Naylor, S. and Wild-Smith, K. (1997) *Broadening Horizons*. Chelmsford: Essex County Council.

Office for Standards in Education (OFSTED) (1996) *The Education of Travelling Children*. London: OFSTED.

Office for Standards in Education (OFSTED) (1999) *Raising the Attainment of Minority Ethnic Pupils*. London: OFSTED.

# CHAPTER 10

# Working with Diverse Communities

*Ann Phoenix*

Many parents in disadvantaged circumstances are passionate about their children's education and see it as a way out of poverty. For a range of reasons, including bad experiences of their own school days, lack of confidence, lack of transport, home, care and employment responsibilities and language and cultural barriers, some parents are not as fully engaged as they, or their children's schools, would like them to be.                    (OFSTED 1999)

## Introduction

It is now accepted that for children to perform optimally in education parents ought to be involved with their children's schools. Parental involvement is also considered to improve rates of school exclusion. In the British context, where schools are now assessed on their examination results and exclusion rates, parental involvement and home–school relations have come to be seen as important to both the academic and the pastoral functioning of schools. To some extent, these have been institutionalised in law, which requires each parent of five–sixteen-year-olds to sign Home–School Agreements (DfEE 1998).

The extensive literature on parental involvement raises questions about whether there are important differences between families that affect their experiences of home–school relations and outcomes for their children. Social class, gender, ethnicity and disability status of children all have an impact on how parents' involvement is viewed by teachers and experienced by parents. While much of the literature examines the effects of parental involvement on children's school attainment, many teachers are at least equally interested in the moderating effects on behaviour that good home–school relations may produce. Of course, school effectiveness, in terms of producing the best results, is linked with both school behaviour and good informal relationships between schools and parents – particularly since behaviour considered consistently difficult by teachers can lead to exclusion from school.

While working with diversity has become almost a catch phrase in education, an examination of the literature on school behaviour, ethnicity and home–school relations indicates that this is, in reality, no more than just a catch phrase. Hardly any research considers the implications of diversity for these issues. This chapter considers some of the background issues that are important to 'working with diversity'. It first discusses parental willingness to support their children's learning, before considering the intersection of ethnicity and constructions of behavioural problems and questioning whether parents can be viewed as partners in the education process. Given the dearth of research available, the chapter offers no prescriptions, but raises issues that need to be considered.

## Willing to support children's learning? Negotiations between parents and teachers

In a comprehensive review of school, family and community links, Dyson and Robson (1999) found that more attention has been paid to how parents can be involved in supporting their children's learning than their effects on their children's behaviour. Since the 1970s there have been consistent findings that children's reading levels can be improved by involving parents in home–school reading schemes (e.g. Tizard *et al.* 1982). These seem to work at least partly because they signal to children that parents are interested in, and agree with, what the school is doing and this improves attitudes to learning. Similar results hold for home–school numeracy schemes.

Regardless of their social class, parents generally welcome initiatives to involve them with their children's learning. The available evidence suggests that 'working class' parents are as keen to be involved as 'middle class' families. This raises a range of issues important to working with diverse communities. Parents bring to their children's schooling their own experiences of having been schoolchildren, while teachers have expectations of which groups of parents value education and with whom it will be easy to collaborate.

The drive towards parental involvement marks an important shift in thinking about the place of parents in their children's education. Teachers used to be considered the 'experts' in education and parents viewed as less expert by comparison and so subject to teachers' views. Today this is less generally accepted. Yet longstanding ideas often continue to have an impact, even as contrary ideas have become widely accepted. Schools, teachers and parents cannot be abstracted from the wider societal context and it is clear that different groups of parents are constructed very differently. An examination of these differences provides an indication of some of the challenges involved when schools attempt to work in partnership with parents in diverse communities, since they illustrate the contradictory possibilities that both teachers and parents bring to their interactions.

## Questions of responsibility

Such a consideration is inextricably linked to the issue of differential educational attainment – an issue about which there has been concern and debate for more than two decades. In the 1980s, the British Government published the Swann Report into the 'underachievement' and high rates of exclusion of black children (then called 'West Indian') in British schools (DES 1985). This report blamed 'the West Indian family' for the school failure of 'West Indian' children on the grounds of high rates of lone motherhood, harsh parental discipline and lack of understanding of the British education system. The Swann Report compared 'Asian' families favourably with 'West Indian' families arguing that their almost universally married, intact families produced the satisfactory educational achievement of Asian children. While this may seem simply statements of facts linked together, it was already known that there were differences within the 'Asian' group in educational performance. Bangladeshi and Mirpuri Pakistani children were not doing well in British schools, although East African Asians and Indian children were achieving well (Rattansi 1992). Work had already been published indicating that for 'West Indians' girls did better than boys and were excluded less frequently (Driver 1980, Fuller 1980).

The interpretation produced in the Swann Report was already common in British society. According to this argument, it was the failing of black parents to control their children adequately or to instil in them acceptable educational and social values that was responsible for their poor behaviour and educational failure. Not surprisingly, parents of Caribbean origin did not share this view. Dissatisfaction with the ways in which British schools and teachers were failing 'West Indian' children generated publications such as *How the West Indian Child is Made Educationally Subnormal in the British School System* (Coard 1971). Such work fuelled the black supplementary school movement that had begun in the 1960s. Black parents and teachers (the vast majority of whom were white British) held competing constructs of each other's responsibilities for black children's poor educational performance. It was a period when integrationist educational philosophies treated people from ethnic groups as if they should adjust to the British school system, rather than vice versa. 'Asian' children were frequently considered 'too passive' in school and their parents blamed for not providing adequate language environments and preventing their daughters from doing physical education (Carby 1982).

## Valuing diversity?

A great deal has changed since the 1970s. Educational philosophies recognise that Britain is multiethnic and many schools have made adaptations to cultural differences by attempting to value all the languages spoken by its pupils and to accommodate differences of religion and other cultural practices. More recent work on 'race', ethnicity and attainment indicates that we need a more complex and sensitive analysis of the issues than that produced in the Swann Report. A survey of 25 British local education authorities (LEAs) conducted by the Office for Standards in Education (OFSTED 1999) found that the performance of all ethnic groups is improving. Bangladeshi, Pakistani, Black Caribbean and Gypsy Traveller children, however, attain poorly in their final secondary school exams (GCSE). Traveller children's performance is the worst and the performance of Black Caribbean children starts well in primary schools, but shows a marked decline in secondary schools. In general girls from minority groups attain more highly than boys.

Gillborn and Mirza (2000) drew on a range of different sources to publish new analyses of 'race', class and gender in educational inequality. Their findings reflected the OFSTED report that inequalities in attainment worsen for African-Caribbean students as they go through secondary school and that social class intersects with ethnicity and gender.

Such findings indicate that 'race', gender, social class and attainment are more complicated, dynamic processes than suggested in the Swann Report. Furthermore, both ethnicity and 'race' are clearly important since different ethnic groups from within the same racial group fare differently, for example African compared to Caribbean people in higher education and Pakistani and Bangladeshi compared to Indian students. It follows that explanations for these results also have to be multi-faceted. The supposed inadequacies of black students and their families hold little explanatory power when, as Gillborn and Gipps (1996) point out, black students have generally been found to be more motivated and less alienated from school than their white peers of the same gender and social class background. Their parents are supportive of education for their children – an idea consistent with the flourishing of supplementary schools as well as schools for teaching parental languages and customs. Despite this evidence to the contrary, there are still indications that some teachers view children from some minority ethnic groups as necessarily having behaviour problems.

## Ethnicity and constructs of behaviour: a case of diversity as deficit?

In 1999, the publication of the MacPherson Report into the flawed investigation into the murder in Britain of a black eighteen-year-old, Stephen Lawrence, drew attention to the prevalence of racism in schools and highlighted the well-documented finding that members of particular ethnic groups are disproportionately excluded from schools.

Tizard *et al.* (1988) found no differences in treatment of black and white children by teachers in their study of infant schools – even though they looked for it. However, there are numerous studies that indicate the prevalence of racism in schools (see the review by Gillborn and Gipps 1996). Some of these studies demonstrate that some teachers do discriminate against black and Asian students – either treating them in stereotypic ways or being hostile towards them.

Most of the research on these issues has been done in secondary schools. However, Carol Ogilvy and her colleagues (1990, 1992) studied nursery staff and children from eight Scottish nursery schools. In half of these schools there was over a third of children from minority ethnic groups, while the other half had less than one sixth of children from minority ethnic groups. Ogilvy *et al.* (1990) reported differences in the way that staff members talked about and treated Asian and white children, which could have an impact on the children's experiences and educational progress, even though some of these differences were subtle. They found a consistent tendency for staff to report that the Asian children had more difficulties than the white Scottish children did. These difficulties were more likely to be reported to be emotional/behavioural rather than cognitive. This interview finding was confirmed by the findings on the behavioural checklist (filled in by head teachers and nursery staff). Language problems that the Asian children had were not recognised.

A study by Sonuga-Barke *et al.* (1993) with slightly older children throws some light on issues of teacher definitions of Asian children as poorly behaved. Sonuga-Barke and his colleagues compared teachers' ratings with 'objective' measures of hyperactivity in Asian and white British boys aged 6 and 7 years of age, who attended schools in London. Boys are more likely than girls to be considered hyperactive by teachers and parents. The objective tests in the study included actometers strapped to the boys' non-dominant wrist and ankle, observations of activity and inattentiveness during a task and a neurological test of clumsiness. The study found that teachers were equally likely to rate white and Asian children as hyperactive, but that the 'Asian' children rated as hyperactive actually had levels of activity and inattention that were no different from the 'English' controls. 'Asian' controls, although rated as being equally as active as 'English' controls, were shown to exhibit much lower levels of activity and inattention than the 'English' controls'.

It was possible that Asian and white children were reacting differently to being in the study. In addition, the original sample was recruited, not by ethnicity, but on the basis of the children's behaviour. In order to overcome these possible confounding factors, a second study was conducted at three local primary schools in southern England (Sonuga-Barke *et al.* 1993). All the Asian boys and an age-matched sample of three times as many white as Asian boys were selected. On the basis of teachers' ratings of the children on Rutter (B2) scales, 10 Asian and 10 white boys were eventually selected to be in the study. Sample children were observed in the classroom and on a standardised auditory vigilance task. As on the first study, in comparison with the observational findings, teachers tended to overestimate Asian boys' hyperactivity so that Asian boys who were rated to be as hyperactive as their white classmates were observed to be less hyperactive in the classroom.

Older children's experiences of racism from their teachers have received more attention than have those of preschool children. Cecile Wright (1992) studied four schools (nursery, first and middle) in one British LEA. She found that 'both Afro-Caribbean and Asian children faced negative teacher interaction in the classroom' (Wright 1992: 100). However, they were subject to different assumptions and hence different treatment. Asian children were expected to have language problems, poor social skills and difficulty interacting with other groups of children in the classroom but they were also expected to be industrious, keen to learn and courteous. African-Caribbean children (particularly boys) were expected to be disruptive in class and were more likely to be the ones singled out for reprimand, even if they were among a group of children behaving in the same way.

This account is from a childcare assistant in the nursery:

The head of the nursery is for ever saying how difficult it is to control the black children in the nursery, because they only responded to being hit . . . there is an attitude that they all get beaten up at home and they're all used to getting a good slap or a punch. There are one or two (black children) that they are quite positive about . . . the black girls they are positive about are thought to be clean, well spoken, lovely personalities. As for the boys . . . who have recently moved into the Reception Class, they were labelled disruptive . . .                          (Wright 1992: 21)

The following exchange, aimed at a black boy by a white teacher, appears to be based on notions that black boys are potential criminals.

Mrs Scott: So you might be visiting him tonight?
Stephen:   [Nods]
Mrs Scott: You're good. I don't think you'll be going to prison [louder, some children in the class look up]. You'll have to remember when you're a man not to fight, steal, throw bricks [pause]. In fact even when you're ten.
Daniel:    Can you go to prison when you're ten?
Mrs Scott: Well, not prison, but you can certainly be taken away.
                                          (Connolly 1995: 173)

Support for the idea that ethnicity and social constructions of behavioural problems are interrelated is provided by an OFSTED (1996) report on exclusions from secondary schools. The evidence indicates that white pupils who are excluded from school are more likely to have experienced trauma and to be below average achievement. They are generally excluded for being verbally abusive to their teachers. Black pupils who were excluded, on the other hand, were more likely to have above average achievement and to have been excluded for challenging their teachers' judgements.

In a period when teachers have been subjected to, and demoralised by, much blame and censure, it is important to point out that many teachers, white and black, have devoted a great deal of time to attempting to eradicate racism and stereotypic judgements (Gillborn 1995). Nonetheless, any attempt to understand the issues involved in working with diverse communities necessarily involves the understanding that there may be difficult and uneven power relations involved. This is particularly the case since parents from ethnic groups are likely to be unwilling to accept teachers' assessments of their children if they believe that their children are viewed differently from those in the majority group.

## Parents in partnership?

A straightforward model of parental involvement requires that parents and teachers come together in a spirit of mutual trust and openness. Yet, it is clear from the above discussion that both parties can bring misconceptions and previous experiences that make for a lack of trust. Miller and Black (2001) conducted a study of 206 children and 30 teachers in almost white schools in northern England. They found that teachers rated parents lower than they rated teachers when it came to judgements about who is likely to be able to provide a solution to pupil's behavioural problems. Indeed, teachers often feel that parents are to blame for children's behavioural problems and this can be communicated to parents, making the home–school relationship tense and difficult. The ethnicity of the parent quoted below is not given.

> I was immensely relieved that my instincts were right and I wasn't just a bad parent. My elation was very short lived. The school queried his diagnosis. It was made patently clear to me that they didn't think there was anything wrong with Damien, and that the problem was with me . . . After fighting for so long for my son, like many parents I came across as overbearing and demanding.                    (Anonymous 1997)

Sykes (2001) did a study of parents, children and teachers in four schools in an inner-London borough where residents come from over 100 countries. She found that 'teachers are not feeling confident about approaching parents, while . . . parents are keen to become more involved in knowing about the school's curriculum' (Sykes 2001: 284). In a study of over 600 parents interviewed in the street in four locations, Thomas and McClelland (1997) also found that parents very much valued getting information from teachers about their children. While Thomas and McClelland do not mention the ethnicity of the parents they interviewed, Sykes identifies this as a factor that affected parental reactions to Home–School Agreements. Many came from 'ethnic-minority families, and it is suggested that the process is particularly helpful to them in that it initiates consultation and helps to clarify issues concerning their child's learning' (Sykes 2001: 282). It may, therefore, be that Home–School Agreements serve to empower parents from a range of different backgrounds.

However, teachers and parents do tend to construct the aims of parental involvement rather differently. Bishop and Swain (2000) conducted a small-scale study of a nurture group for pupils with EBD in a primary school in an impoverished inner-city area. They found that a major difficulty in establishing parental involvement as a partnership was that parents and teachers had different constructions of the relevant issues:

> The main concern for these parents was the provision of support to maintain their child in a mainstream school, and from their viewpoint involvement was about supporting the school in this. Whereas the main

concern for teachers was the management and control of the class, and parental involvement is about engaging parents in nurturing control at home. It seems too that the source of the problem from the teachers' viewpoint can be the child or the child's disruptive behaviour, whereas from the parents' viewpoint it can be the teaching/learning environment in mainstream classes that is crucial.        (Bishop and Swain 2000: 30)

Not only do teachers often blame parents for problems in children's behaviour, after successful collaborative home–school interventions they tend not to consider that parents have played an important part in bringing about positive change (Miller and Black 2001).

Dyson and Robson (1999) suggest that their review of the literature tells us little about why some parental involvement schemes are unsuccessful or the reasons that some schools, teachers and parents drop out of schemes or do not participate at all. They suggest that the model of parent–child relations and of family values embedded in the parental involvement movement may devalue the values and childrearing practices of families who are already marginalised. This may then have the effect of alienating such families.

It is now well documented that working class parents often find it harder to engage in school negotiations with teachers than do middle class parents, particularly those who have themselves been well educated and are in professional jobs (Salmon 1998). A study by Ribbens (1993) indicates how white working class mothers, who are keen to have contact with their children's teachers, can experience such contacts as hostile because they have different expectations:

While the teachers have made their views clear to Janet, she has not vocalised her reactions to them, implying an inequality of power between them. Janet does not regard herself as playing a major educational role, even though she is willing to undertake educational tasks under the teachers' direction . . . Dealing with the school thus carries much potential for tension, because even though there may be agreement about the importance of learning, there may be different conceptions of the *nature of the child* concerned, and of the *role of the teacher* . . . The boundary between home and school is here quite sharply defined, with the potential for considerable tensions in mother–teacher relationships unless these are carefully managed, despite goodwill on both sides.

(Ribbens 1993: 98)

Some teachers also feel that parents cannot support their children's learning because of their own poor educational background. They therefore expect parents to support them (the teachers) as experts on their own terms with parents ensuring that children have the necessary equipment to do their work and do their homework. In the school studied by Crozier (1999) teachers were successful in maintaining the lay–professional boundaries with working class parents. From the parents' accounts, they recognised that teachers got fed up with parents who were 'pushy' and considered that the school should be left to get on with its job without interference from parents.

The issues raised by the power imbalance between parents and teachers are equally relevant to a consideration of parents from minority ethnic groups (a high proportion of whom come from the working classes). The situation is exacerbated because parents from particular groups are well aware that their children do not do well at school. As a result, they do not necessarily start from a position of trust in relation to schools. In a study of ten–thirteen-year-old children's out of school lives, Petrie *et al.* (2000) found that:

> Many mothers from ethnic minority groups reported either that their children had tutors, went to supplementary schools and/or that they themselves supervised homework and indeed set it when they thought the school's part was inadequate.                    (Petrie *et al.* 2000: 48)

## Issues for collaboration on behaviour

It was not only education *per se* that these parents from ethnic minority groups reported they were unhappy about. Many considered that schools did not promote key values of discipline and respect for adults that they valued, as for example in this quote from a Sikh father in the Petrie *et al.* study:

> The schools don't teach the children how to behave, so one cannot expect the play centre to teach the children how to behave properly. If they did then parents wouldn't be so upset. The children know how to respect their elders, to respect their parents. These people don't know about these things, these things the schools don't teach.
>                    (Petrie *et al.* 2000: 49)

It is not that teachers do not recognise cultural differences between themselves and parents, but that they devalue difference and diversity. Crozier (1999: 326) quotes the deputy head from the secondary school she studied: 'I think sometimes teachers can . . . be a bit off-hand . . . a bit dismissive because a parent perhaps comes from . . . a different background themselves, and certainly many of our parents do . . .' Such dismissiveness can be exacerbated if parents are not fluent in English.

Parents from ethnic groups can be only too aware that schools not only do not reflect their values, but also do not respect them. It is this idea that is powerfully expressed by the Bangladeshi mother of a deaf son when she says: 'I send my child to school and he comes back an Englishman' (Ahmad *et al.* 2000: 71).

Given this potential gulf between teachers' and parents' constructions, it is perhaps not surprising that parents may distrust what schools and teachers say about their children. This may be partly because parents feel that teachers are not on their side and there is a gulf of incomprehension between home and school, but it can also be because children are different in different contexts (as are adults). In a longitudinal study of children from nursery to the end of infant school, Tizard *et al.* (1988) found that many black boys came to be viewed as boisterous or on the verge of behavioural problems. However, their parents did not experience them in this way. It would, therefore, have been puzzling and incredible for them to be told that their children were badly behaved. It is not being suggested that children from ethnic groups never have behavioural problems. Clearly some do and over the course of school careers, some – particularly black boys – can become challenging to teachers in response to what they perceive as racism from teachers (Mac an Ghaill 1988, Sewell 1997).

The issue of racism and negative social constructions by teachers, however, continue to make it difficult for teachers and parents from these groups to collaborate on dealing with children's behavioural problems. It is not being suggested that all teachers construct parents and children from minority groups as problematic. Gillborn (1995) studied three secondary schools in different parts of Britain. In two of these schools, at least half of the pupils were from South Asian backgrounds and the third, while predominantly white, drew about 15 per cent of their students from ethnic groups. These schools were committed to antiracist policies and various members of staff had put a lot of work into developing antiracist strategies. In doing so, they had managed to gain support from white parents. Nevertheless, Gillborn found that a small minority of teachers express generalised views that depict African-Caribbean students (as a group) as a greater threat to their authority.

> I think there is a problem with Afro-Caribbean girls in this school . . . I am not sure how to handle them, how to cope. You try not to sound racist, but some of them are very lively. They have got a lot to offer. I

have one in my tutor group with whom a lot of the time I don't get on very well . . .                                                          (Gillborn 1995: 183)

In his earlier work, Gillborn (1990) found that teachers' expectations that children of African-Caribbean origin automatically constituted disciplinary problems led to the possibility of escalating conflicts and poor relations – a finding consistent with those from Sewell's (1997) study of black secondary school boys.

Nehaul (1996) conducted a study of 25 children of Caribbean origin and five of their teachers. They attended primary schools in the British Midlands that were renowned for being concerned to ensure that there were equal opportunities for black children. She found that the teachers considered that 16 of the 25 parents were interested in their children's academic development and supportive to the school. There appeared to be satisfactory contacts with the parents of another three children and only in three cases were there concerns expressed about the support provided by parents. The five teachers studied by Nehaul did not express generally negative perceptions of children from minoritised ethnic groups comparable to the teacher quoted by Gillborn. She argues (Nehaul 1996: 83) that 'Teachers were not advocating or subscribing to a deficit theory about families and homes . . . teachers did not assume that families were problematic because of their Caribbean backgrounds.' Despite this, teachers mentioned poor behaviour as a cause for concern in relation to 17 of the 25 pupils and good behaviour for only two.

## The way forward?

This chapter started by reiterating currently prevailing attitudes that parental involvement in their children's education is important both for children's well-being and as a panacea against educational failure and behavioural problems. Yet, it has largely focused on barriers to such involvement in terms of the resistance of some teachers to allowing parents power in the teacher–parent relationship. For parents from ethnic groups, the chapter also highlighted the continued propensity for some teachers to construct difference and diversity as deficit. However, it has also indicated that there are schools and teachers where such negative stereotyping is not prevalent and school–home relations are more collaborative. A fair amount is known about what works in general. For example:

Addressing ethnic minority underachievement requires a whole-school approach. Case studies have highlighted the positive potential of school-based change on ethnic minority achievement. Effective schools involve teachers, pupils and the local community in re-evaluating the school ethos. Equality, anti-bullying and racial harassment policies can also make a difference. Good practice guidance helps but a more proactive approach is required and schools should be offered the direct additional support of individuals who are experienced and successful in raising the attainment of ethnic minority pupils (see earlier recommendation on Schools Plus Teams and supplementary and mother tongue teaching).

(OFSTED 1999)

Gillborn (1995) also identified the importance of whole-school approaches to disrupting racism and teachers' negative stereotypes of children from certain groups.

Realistically, we should not be surprised that some teachers still hold negative and essentialist views despite the wealth of antiracist work in Seacole. The school had achieved a great deal but it is utopian to expect total success, especially in the face of such deeply rooted stereotypes. This testifies to the need consistently to address such views on a school-wide basis, for example, as part of inservice and policy review work.

(Gillborn 1995: 183)

Gillborn's work highlights the importance of viewing change in schools as possible and as part of a process that shifts power relations. This shift in power relations requires that parents' concerns are taken seriously, rather than brushed aside, so that parents can be involved with their children's education without having to express themselves forcibly in order to be heard. Parents also need to be thoroughly informed about the curriculum and have a chance to have some input where appropriate. This may involve the encouragement of parents' groups – perhaps for parents from particular ethnic groups – and possibly the use of the school for training courses for parents themselves (NIACE 1997).

Some schools have already established home–school liaison teams and employed liaison teachers. The outreach work that this permits is crucially important given that we know that many parents from minority ethnic groups work in the poorest paid sectors of the economy with the least flexible working conditions. In addition, issues of fluency in English make it important that teachers have access to translators fluent in the languages of the community served by the school. A study by Song (1999) of children of Chinese origin in Britain indicates how little time parents have away from their takeaway restaurant businesses. In consequence, invitations to such parents to come into schools could not possibly be successful.

## Summary

There is currently little research available that directly addresses the school behaviour of children from minority ethnic groups and teacher–parents' collaboration about this. Given the wealth of evidence that suggests that some teachers find this a difficult area of their work and hold negative stereotypes of particular groups, there is an urgent need for research in this area. Such research would need to address the complexities of gender, and social class together with commonalities and differences within and across ethnic groups.

## References

Ahmad, W. *et al.* (2000) '"I send my child to school and he comes back an Englishman": minority ethnic deaf people, identity politics and services', in Ahmad, W. (ed.) *Ethnicity, Disability and Chronic Illness*, 67–84. Buckingham: Open University Press.

Anonymous (1997) 'AD/HD: two parents tell their personal stories', *Emotional and Behavioural Difficulties* **2**(2), 25–9.

Bishop, A. and Swain, J. (2000) 'Early years education and children with behavioural and emotional difficulties: nurturing parental involvement?', *Emotional and Behavioural Difficulties* **5**(4), 26–31.

Carby, H. (1982) 'Schooling in Babylon', in Centre for Contemporary Cultural Studies *The Empire Strikes Back: Race and racism in 70s Britain*, 183–211. London: Hutchinson.

Coard, B. (1971) *How the West Indian Child is Made Educationally Subnormal in the British School System*. London: New Beacon Books.

Connolly, P. (1995) 'Boys will be boys? Racism, sexuality and the construction of masculine identities among infant boys', in Holland, J. and Blair, M. (eds) *Equality and Difference: Debates and issues in feminist research and pedagogy*. Clevedon: Multilingual Matters.

Crozier, G. (1999) 'Is it a case of "We know when we're not wanted"? The parents' perspective on parent–teacher roles and relationships', *Educational Research* **41**(3), 315–28.

Department for Education and Employment (DfEE) (1998) *Home–School Agreements: What every parent should know*. Online: http://www.dfee.gov.uk/, accessed 28 August 2001.

Department of Education and Science (DES) (1985) *Education for All: The report of the Committee of Inquiry into the Education of Children from Ethnic Minority Groups*. Chairman Lord Swann. London: The Stationery Office.

Driver, G. (1980) *Beyond Underachievement*. London: Commission for Racial Equality.

Dyson, A. and Robson, E. (1999) *School, Family, Community: Mapping school inclusion in the UK*. Leicester: National Youth Agency and Joseph Rowntree Foundation.

Fuller, M. (1980) 'Black girls in a London comprehensive', in Deem, R. (ed.) *Schooling for Women's Work*, 52–65. London: Routledge and Kegan Paul.

Gillborn, D. (1990) *'Race', Ethnicity and Education: Teaching and learning in multiethnic schools*. London: Unwin Hyman.

Gillborn, D. (1995) *Racism and Antiracism in Real Schools*. Buckingham: Open University Press.

Gillborn, D. and Gipps, C. (1996) *Recent Research on Achievements of Ethnic Minority Pupils*. Report for the Office for Standards in Education. London: HMSO.

Gillborn, D. and Mirza, H. S. (2000) *Educational Inequality: Mapping race, class and gender. A synthesis of evidence*. London: OFSTED.

Mac an Ghaill, M. (1988) *Young, Gifted and Black*. Milton Keynes: Open University Press.

MacPherson, W. (1999) *The Stephen Lawrence Inquiry*. CM 4262–1. London: The Stationery Office.

Miller, A. and Black, L. (2001) 'Does support for home–school behaviour plans exist within teacher and pupil cultures?', *Educational Psychology in Practice*, **17**(3), 245–61.

National Institute of Adult Continuing Education (NIACE) (1997) *Learning to Live in a Multi-Cultural Society: Home–school liaison*. Leicester: NIACE.

Nehaul, K. (1996) *The Schooling of Children of Caribbean Heritage*. Stoke-on-Trent: Trentham.

Office for Standards in Education (OFSTED) (1996) *Exclusions from Secondary Schools*. London: OFSTED.

Office for Standards in Education (OFSTED) (1999) 'Raising the Attainment of Ethnic Minority Pupils', in Schools Plus Policy Action Team 11 (2000) *Improving the Educational Chances of Children and Young People from Disadvantaged Areas*. London: DfEE. Online: http://www.dfee.gov.uk/schools-plus/, accessed 28 August 2001.

Ogilvy, C. *et al*. (1990) 'Staff attitudes and perceptions in multi-cultural nursery schools', *Early Child Development and Care* **64**, 1–13.

Ogilvy, C. *et al*. (1992) 'Staff–child interaction styles in multi-ethnic nursery schools', *British Journal of Developmental Psychology* **10**, 85–97.

Petrie, P. *et al*. (2000) *Out-of-School Lives, Out-of-School Services*. London: The Stationery Office.

Rattansi, A. (1992) 'Changing the subject? Racism, culture and education', in Donald, J. and Rattansi, A. (eds) *'Race', Culture and Difference*, 11–48. London: Sage.

Ribbens, J. (1993) 'Having a word with the teacher: Ongoing negotiations across home–school boundaries', in David, M. *et al*. (eds) *Mothers and Education: Inside out?*, 91–126. London: Macmillan.

Salmon, P. (1998) *Life at School: Education and psychology*. London: Constable.

Sewell, T. (1997) *Black Masculinities and Schooling: How black boys survive modern schooling*. Stoke on Trent: Trentham Books.

Song, M. (1999) *Helping Out: Children's labor in ethnic businesses*. Philadelphia: Temple University Press.

Sonuga-Barke, E. *et al*. (1993) 'Inter-ethnic bias in teachers' ratings of childhood hyperactivity', *British Journal of Developmental Psychology* **11**, 187–200.

Sykes, G. (2001) 'Home–school agreements: A tool for parental control or for partnership?', *Educational Psychology in Practice* **17**(3), 273–86.

Thomas, G. and McClelland, R. (1997) 'Parents in a market place: Some responses to information, diversity and power', *Educational Research* **39**(2), 185–94.

Tizard, B. *et al*. (1988) *Young Children at School in the Inner City*. London: Lawrence Erlbaum.

Tizard, J. *et al*. (1982) 'Symposium: Reading. Collaboration between teachers and parents in assisting children's reading', *British Journal of Educational Psychology* **52**(1) 1–15.

Wright, C. (1992) *Race Relations in the Primary School*. London: David Fulton Publishers.

CHAPTER 11

# Solution Focused Approaches to Promote Effective Home–School Partnerships

*Elizabeth Gillies*

## Introduction

This chapter is about creating effective conversations between school and home. We can often find ourselves in conversations that go round and round talking about problems leaving everyone involved feeling negative, hopeless and helpless. Sometimes this kind of over-analysis leads to complete paralysis. 'If the problem is so big what on earth can I try to do about it?' We can, however, choose to talk in different ways that are more optimistic and respectful. Solution Focused Brief Therapy (SFBT) offers options that focus our perceptions, thoughts and language on exploring competencies and solutions rather than exploring problems.

There is a growing literature on solution focused work in schools (Durrant 1993, Rhodes and Ajmal 1995, Ajmal and Rees 2001). These offer excellent reading for those interested in exploring these ideas further. There are many examples of how the theory and language of therapy can be successfully used to inform thinking and work in schools and, as such, the term solution focused thinking will be used in this chapter as well as of Solution Focused Brief Therapy.

The focus in this chapter is about the interface between home and schools in relation to behaviour and what solution focused thinking has to offer.

These two scenarios of parent–teacher meetings detail the different conversations that might take place:

### Parent–teacher scenario 1

Teacher:   John had a terrible day in school again today. It all started almost the moment he arrived in class. He hit one of the children and spent most of the day out of class. I really can't have him doing this in school. He just cannot concentrate on anything and won't listen. He is rude to me. Why is he doing this?

Parent:   Well, at home he is fine. He listens to me most of the time. You know he is not a bad kid, he's just lively sometimes and needs a lot of love. He really likes coming to school and he is always eager to come.

Teacher:   Well, he is now finding it difficult to get on with the other children. I think they are a bit afraid of him because he hits out. He comes into the class very unhappy and things don't really improve. I am really surprised that he does like coming to school. And now some of the other parents have started to complain and something must be done.

Parent:   What are you going to do? Will John be excluded? I don't want that to happen. I think you just need to give him some time and attention and he will be fine.

Teacher:   I already give John much more time than any other pupil does in the class and I really can't give him more. What I want you to do is to bring him into the class in a happy mood. That would give us all a much better start.

Parent:   But I think we do come to school in a happy mood. I don't think I can do anything else. This seems to be a problem in the school.

Teacher:   John needs to be happy coming into school and you have control over that. If you cannot make him happy before school then I can only see that things will get worse . . .

## Parent–teacher scenario 2

Teacher:   Thanks for making this time available for us to talk. It was good that you managed to sort out some childminding for John's brother.

Parent:   I have some good neighbours and we all help each other out. Sometimes you just need a bit of time to get things done so we are all good at offering help when we can. Even though our children are all quite different ages they seem to get along together fairly well.

Teacher:   That sounds an excellent arrangement that you have managed to set up. You are right that we all just need a bit of time to get things done on our own. It will really help us to have some uninterrupted time together today. Thanks. We all had a terrible day in school today. It all started almost the moment John

|          |                                                                                                                                                                                                                                                    |
|----------|----------------------------------------------------------------------------------------------------------------------------------------------------------------------------------------------------------------------------------------------------|
|          | arrived in class. He hit one of the children and spent most of the day out of class. We need to think together about how we can improve this situation. What do you think you would like to get from our meeting today?                             |
| Parent:  | Well, I hadn't really thought about that but I do want John to behave at school. You know he is not a bad kid, he's just lively sometimes and needs a lot of love. He really likes coming to school and he is always eager to come.                 |
| Teacher: | I want similar things from the meeting too. He has been lively sometimes. I want him to be more settled, especially at the beginning of the day. I also want him to be able to play with the other children. Do you think we should concentrate on his behaviour first? |
| Parent:  | Yes, that sounds the best place to start.                                                                                                                                                                                                          |
| Teacher: | Let's start off with thinking about what is working. How do you cope with him?                                                                                                                                                                     |
| Parent:  | I say to him, I want you to go to school. I want you to learn to read and he really does want to read. I think he finds reading difficult as he sees all the other children reading.                                                               |
| Teacher: | So he wants to read?                                                                                                                                                                                                                                |
| Parent:  | Yes, I know he does. He asks me to read with him at home and I try to read to him as often as I can. When we sit and read together he listens well, and believe it or not he is still!                                                             |
| Teacher: | So you have found a way to have some quiet time together, that is great. I wonder if we could do something like that in school?                                                                                                                    |
| Parent:  | What do you mean?                                                                                                                                                                                                                                   |
| Teacher: | Well, I am interested in the way that you have found to have a quiet time with John and how settled he is when someone reads to him. I wonder if there is anyone in school that might be able to read with him first thing in the morning. Who do you think would be the best person? . . . |

Although these two scenarios are fictional, perhaps we have all been in similar situations where some actions and words facilitate a supportive interaction while others, though trying to fix the problem, create a negative blaming dialogue. It is likely that parents and teachers would prefer the second scenario as it takes account of all views and ideas and creates a positive interaction.

## What makes the conversation solution focused?

Solution Focused Brief Therapy is an approach developed over the last 20 years by Steve de Shazer and his colleagues in the USA. The main ideas are encapsulated in the title: firstly the focus is on solutions and secondly the length of contact between therapist and client is expected to be short. Each session is viewed as the first and last time.

It can be easy to view SFBT as some very useful questions but it is more than this. It is a way of *viewing and doing*. It is about the assumptions we make about the problem, about our belief systems, and then about the conversations we create. Viewing and doing are **both** needed. How we perceive the world affects what we say and do. Let's consider our assumptions first.

What assumptions do you hold about children and parents who are experiencing behavioural difficulties? How do you make sense of behavioural problems?

> The child's behaviour can be blamed on someone . . . either the child themselves, the parents or even the *teacher* . . . **or** . . . the issues are best viewed as patterns maintained by all involved in attempts to solve the problem.

> Nothing can be done to change the behaviour, especially if a label has been given, for example Attention Deficit Hyperactivity Disorder (ADHD) . . . **or** . . . the behaviours causing concern are not constant. There are exceptions, times that the behaviour does not happen or happens less than usual.

> Once the reasons and causes are understood then and only then can the problem be 'fixed' . . . **or** . . . it is more helpful to explore solutions rather than trying to understand the cause.

> The only way to change the problem behaviour is to change the pupil's behaviour . . . **or** . . . using the strengths, resources and exploring what is working with everyone that is key to the issue will uncover possible options for change. (Adapted from Durrant 1993)

If your responses tended more towards the second options, then perhaps you already hold solution focused assumptions.

## What can shape our work with parents?

Research from Lambert (1992), which is written up in Murphy and Duncan (1997), points to the key factors that led to change in a large sample of thousands of clients and hundreds of practitioners with broad-ranging problems in different settings. It is an extremely helpful piece of research that reveals what works in supporting people with difficulties. The research is also referred to in Stephenson and Johal-Smith (2001) who found this a helpful model for working in schools.

## Key factors for successful intervention

The largest contributor to the change process was **client factors** at 40 per cent. Client factors included what the client was already doing well and what other resources they had that could be tapped, for example their skills and interests. Who they could call on for support and help and their ability to embrace change were also important.

Researchers defined the **relationship factors** as empathy, warmth, acceptance and encouragement of risk taking. These factors accounted for 30 per cent in the change process.

Changes and improvements resulted in part from **placebo factors** (15 per cent). Just being hopeful about change can bring about change.

**Model factors** accounted for 15 per cent of what was effective about the intervention. This referred to the theory and technique of the practitioner. Utilising findings from research about the things that contribute to successful interventions was important, as was ensuring the approach was acceptable for the client.

## *So what do we learn from this?*

Paying great attention to the skills and resources that parents bring with them needs to be high on our agenda.

- Creating respectful relationships with parents is essential.
- We need to attend to our feelings about the problem. Do we think we can make a difference?
- Questioning our approach is important. Does it actually help make the difference we want? Is our approach acceptable for our clients?

All the above principles are not necessarily new, but what solution focused thinking brings is a coherent way to maximise the factors we know make a difference.

Let's explore each of these factors in turn and see what solution focused thinking has to offer.

## Client factors: mobilising skills and resources

If we want changes to occur in behaviour then we have to explore the resources and strengths that are there, if only we dare ask. In the second parent–teacher scenario above, the resources were acknowledged and uncovered by asking the question: 'How do you cope with him?' This question demonstrates to the parent a belief that they are doing something that is working. Even though there is a problem there are times when there is no problem or it is less. There are difficulties *and* there are strengths.

The question also emphasises partnership; the teacher is open and willing to learn from the parent. This enhances the cooperation between home and school. Equally the teacher could have asked: 'When are the better days? What is different about these times? What do I do that makes it different?' Teachers and parents can find it difficult to remind themselves of their strengths when problems dominate.

'What else?' questions are also useful, as they uncover more resources and focus on the solutions that already exist. 'And what else do you do to cope with him?' 'What else do you do that settles him?' Parents usually have a wide range of tactics and are aware of their outcomes.

---

# Case study: Mobilising skills

I was once involved with a preschool setting, a four-year-old and his parents. The problem was framed as 'The adults involved found him demanding and difficult to control. At times he could be aggressive towards other children.' I asked his mother what interests and skills she had. The staff were surprised as they had tended to view her as a mum who was unable to cope and she was ready to believe this of herself too. It happened that this parent was an expert dog trainer. She had trained her own dogs successfully and had helped other people do so. In our discussions she demonstrated her knowledge and skills in this area. I wondered aloud how these skills could be used with her son. The mother easily saw some connections and was able to plan what she would try with her son. The result was a positive one for home and school.

---

O'Hanlon (1999) describes this as 'importing some solution patterns from other situations in which you feel competent'. From this example it is clear that the skills do not have to be directly related to the problem. It is the subsequent exploration of how these skills could be used that is important. Asking about skills and resources is particularly important with parents who often feel responsible and blamed for their child's behaviour. They need to be reminded of their skills and areas where they are competent.

## Constructive feedback

Towards the end of the session there is usually a break to think about the content of the meeting and provide constructive feedback. This is another way to amplify the skills and resources of the participants in the meeting. These might be the parents' skills and also what went well in the meeting. Perhaps asking a question or discussing a particular topic helped make a difference. For example:

> 'I want to say how impressed I am that you have taken the trouble to organise uninterrupted time to help think about the problem with me. It seems to me that you have a good relationship with your son and have discovered some good ways to relax together. Talking about this has helped me think about how we can use what is working with you at home and try it out in school . . .'

Constructive feedback can also be written and sent as a letter. These are permanent reminders of what is working and the solutions that were discussed in the meeting. It can be rare to receive good news in writing, so letters can make a big and long-lasting impression. Parents really appreciate them.

## Mobilising skills and resources

First believe parents are doing their best and that they have expertise.

- Explore skills and resources at work, in interests, with friends and other contexts. These skills may be from the past, some that are current or those that might be.
- Explore how solution patterns can be imported into the problem situation.
- Think about what feedback to provide and how to do it.

Some useful questions are:

> 'Tell me what are you good at.'
> 'How do you like to spend your free time?'
> 'What have you learnt from _____ that would help in this problem?'

## Relationship factors: building partnerships

For some time partnership with parents has been regarded as good and necessary practice in schools (Wolfendale 1997, DfEE 2000). Many schools acknowledge this, though there can still be a gap in perceptions between schools and parents. Solution focused thinking has much to offer in *how* to create cooperative relationships.

Think of the last meeting you had with a parent. What dominated – problems or solutions? What kind of relationship did you establish? And how did you do this? Perhaps you used some of the following skills.

### Problem-free talk

How did the conversation begin? Did it start as in the first parent–teacher scenario straight away with the problem or was there some problem-free talk first? In the second parent–teacher scenario there was problem-free talk about the parent managing to arrange childcare for the meeting. The parent was thanked for managing to do this and at the same time certain resources were uncovered. The parent had developed a good network of other parents who helped each other out. Problem-free talk helps to underline that the person is more than the problem. Again there are problems *and* there are strengths. In the problem-free talk part of the meeting it is useful to think about what skills and resources the parent is demonstrating; for example the parent is putting their child's needs high on their agenda by making arrangements for her younger children so she can have an uninterrupted discussion.

### What will we talk about?

It is useful to think about who set the agenda and how much others contributed and shaped the discussion. In the second parent–teacher scenario, the teacher asked the parent what they wanted from the meeting. There was an agreement on what they would work on together. This meeting was then jointly owned with a greater equality in the relationship.

In consultations with teachers it has been useful to provide some questions to think about before the consultation (Wagner and Gillies 2001). Preparation for the meeting gives it importance. For example:

- What do you hope to get from the consultation?
- What are the child's positive abilities, interests and attitudes?
- What concerns you about this pupil?
- What strategies have you already tried?

- What effects have you noted?
- When does the behaviour you want happen?
- What is different about these times?
- What other relevant information would you like to share?

It is important to think carefully about appropriate questions for parents and the language used. Providing some framework for the meeting, especially about what parents want to get out of it, demonstrates willingness for partnership work.

## Goals: what do people want to happen?

Uncovering goals is important in solution focused thinking. How will you get somewhere if you don't know where you are going? And how will you know when you have arrived?

Negotiating goals is critical to the process of solution focused thinking. Both parties will have some ideas about what they want to get out of the meeting and both sides need to be heard. In the second parent–teacher scenario, the teacher asked the parent, 'What do you think you would like to get out of the meeting today?' The teacher listened to the parent and then was able to share her own goals. They agreed on what they would work on first. In reality arriving at the goals might not be as quick as this. Therefore the time spent on eliciting goals and agreeing the focus of the conversation at the beginning of the meeting is critical.

De Shazer (1991) offers some guidance on what are the qualities of well-formed goals. They should be:

- salient
- small rather than large
- described in specific, concrete behavioural terms
- described as the start of something, not the end of something
- involving new behaviour rather than the absence or cessation of old behaviour
- perceived as involving hard work
- achievable within a practical context of home and work.

When faced with behavioural difficulties we often want a complete turn-around. We want the behaviour to stop, though we may not have thought about the steps towards this or the behaviour we want instead. The above points remind us to start small as small changes create ripples and lead to bigger changes. Thinking of the behaviour we want 'instead' focuses us back to our goals.

'I want him to stop being rude to me.'
'What behaviour would you like to see instead?'
'I want him to smile at me.'

The reply then can lead you into talking about the times he has smiled (see Exploring exceptions on page 152).

Some other useful goal questions are:

'How would you know that it was worthwhile coming to the meeting today?'
'If this had been a really good meeting, what would be different?'

## The miracle question

This is a question, with follow-on questions, designed to explore a description of a day without the problem. It emphasises and separates the difference between problems and solutions. Creating solutions is not automatically related to the problem (de Shazer 1985).

'Suppose, you go home tonight and go to sleep, and while asleep a miracle happens. The problems you had are solved, but you don't know it happened. When you wake up tomorrow, how will you discover the miracle has happened?'
'What difference would that make for you?'
'How would you respond?'
'When have little pieces of the miracle happened already?'

These questions are the start of a process of exploration about what life would be like without the problem.

Teachers might be able to ask themselves these questions in the meeting. 'If you had asked me that question my reply would have been . . .'

## Where do solutions come from?

One of the major differences between the two parent–teacher scenarios is the origin of the solution. In the first scenario the teacher gave what she felt was some useful advice to the parent. This was the teacher's solution with little ownership from the parent. This clearly didn't really fit with the solution of the parent. Some work with teachers, on their experience of receiving advice in role play, consistently reported they felt belittled, inadequate, useless and thought others viewed them as inferior (Gillies 2000). This is a major warning against thinking that you have the perfect solution, if only the parent would do it. People like and are more persuaded by their own solutions rather than the ones given to them.

## Powerful words

In the second scenario there was evidence that the teacher was listening to the parent by using the parent's language: 'just need a bit of time', 'he is lively sometimes'. Small, though significant, details like this go a long way to increasing cooperation. Asking about how the parent copes, because after all they are with their child more and know their child best, is a way of 'accusing the parent of doing something right' (de Shazer 1996).

## Building partnerships

To build a partnership:

- connect with the parent and not the problem
- talk about goals and be clear about what they will be from the parents' viewpoint and the schools'
- agree on some well-formed goals, or the closest you can get
- think about giving advice before you do it
- above all else, listen and show you are listening.

## Placebo influences: harnessing hope

Hope and expectancy that change will occur are potent factors in promoting more change. When both parents and teachers hope that change will happen this will influence the process.

Think of the last meeting that you had with a parent and use these scaling questions to help you explore your hopefulness. Before the meeting, how hopeful were you that you would work out a solution together? Use a scale of 0–10, with 0 being the point of no hope and 10 the point of high optimism. Place yourself at one point on this line.

- What would it take for you to be one point higher?
- What difference do you think this would make to you?
- What difference do you think this would make to the parent/s?
- Where do you think the parent/s would place themselves on the scale?
- What do you think they would say would make them one point higher on the scale?

Murphy and Duncan (1997) acknowledge the fact that teachers and parents often seek help when a crisis point is reached. During these times it is very difficult to believe that a positive change can happen, yet we know this is a crucial factor.

Creating 'positive stories' that bring hope is central to solution focused thinking. Here are a few examples.

## Exploring exceptions

Often we can hold an all or nothing view of a problem, especially so in relation to behavioural difficulties:

'He just cannot concentrate on anything and won't listen.'
'He is rude to me.'

Yet we know that the exact same behaviour does not always happen in exactly the same ways. There are exceptions, that is, times when the behaviour did not occur at all or did so with less intensity. Perhaps, even some positive behaviour occurred, the behaviour that you did want. It can be easy to overlook these desired behaviours and even regard them as a fluke. These flukes do not fit in with the all or nothing view of the unwanted behaviour. Therefore it is important to pay attention to the phrases that reveal exceptions:

'He listens to me *most* of the time.'
'He's just lively *sometimes*.'

These words lead us to think about what happens when the behaviour we want is there:

'So what is different about the times when he listens?'
'What else?'
'What do you do differently?'
'Who else was involved?'
'What differences did they notice?'
'How did you get that to happen?'
'How could you do more of that?'

Finding and exploring exceptions brings hope in noticing the times that things are going well. The exploration provides clues to recreate the specific set of circumstances that promotes solutions.

## The miracle question

As previously described the miracle question is a way of clarifying goals and it is also a way of anticipating change. Talking about miracles and imagining life without the problem boosts hope. Discussing details about the miracle makes the dreamed-about possibility more a reality. There might even have been times that the miracle or part of it has already happened. Asking the miracle question seems to distance the person from the problem and look to a place where other things are possible.

## Scaling questions

Scaling questions, like the ones described above, offer the notion that things can and do change. There is nothing like noticing and measuring change to create more change. Scaling questions are versatile, simple and provide us with the expectation that change will occur: 'like words, numbers are magic' (de Shazer 1994).

Scaling questions can provide ways of noting progress from one meeting to the next. I remember a parent coming into the school for a follow-up meeting and excitedly reporting they were now a 7. They had been able to move up 4 points on their scale. This was success. One family who had some issues with their son's behaviour had English as their second language. Drawing the scale for them provided a visual way of representing the problem and a basis for change.

Here is a scaling script to help teachers think about an issue in their classroom. It might be useful to think of an issue and then work through the questions.

On a scale of 0–10, with 0 being the worst position in relation to the issue and 10 representing perhaps the day after the miracle, where are you now?

What moved you from 0 to this point? (There is an assumption here that very few people say they are at 0.)

What would be happening if you were one point higher on the scale?

What would you be doing differently?

What is the highest point you have reached?

What helped this to happen?

Where would be good enough on the scale?

How come things are not worse?

What would be the first steps to get to the next point on the scale?

How confident are you on a scale of 0–10 that this would work? What would make you more confident?

When you have given some time to this think about your experience. How did this affect your hope and plans that there could be answers and that you have them? What do you think you could use in your parent–teacher meetings?

### Our hopeful language

The words we use hold great meaning about our view of the world. We can use words that open up possibilities for change and create the feeling that a better future is possible. O'Hanlon (1999) calls this 'possibility talk' and 'positive expectancy talk'. Here are some examples.

- Use the past tense to describe the problem: 'He has been lively.' This implies there can be a change of behaviour in the future. The problem is not viewed as static.
- Use words that suggest exceptions: 'Usually he finds it difficult to settle down in class.' 'Sometimes he has some difficulties sharing with other children.'
- Think about the difference between these phrases: 'What have you done that has been successful?' **or** 'Have you done anything that has been successful?' The first implies competence and certainty that there have been successful times. The second questions whether indeed anything has worked and is much less hopeful. 'When things improve I will . . .' **or** 'If things improve I will . . .' The first phrase assumes the situation will improve while the second introduces some doubt about success.

### Harnessing hope

Believe that you and the parent can make a difference. Think about how to use questions and words to create a positive hopeful story.

## Model factors: employing effective theories

This brings us back to the start of the chapter where we explored our assumptions, our theories about behaviour and working with parents. It is one thing to have assumptions and another to know that they are effective in bringing about change. In our busy lives and with the difficulties that behavioural problems bring, we need to employ methods that are effective and are workable within our school settings.

Due to the growing interest in Solution Focused Brief Therapy there is increasing research about the outcomes of this approach. McKeel (1999) reviewed a body of SFBT work that looked at effectiveness, and what was helpful from the practitioners' view and clients' view. The evidence reported was that SFBT is effective 'for a broad range' of difficulties. Gingerich and Eisengart (2000) also report success comparable with other types of approaches, with SFBT sometimes taking less time.

People using SFBT report the techniques are easy to use (McKeel 1999); however, the techniques alone are not enough. The assumptions are also needed.

Clients who were involved in SFBT have reported they 'appreciate the questions . . . the SFBT focus on strengths, noticing differences, focusing on what works and the positive atmosphere'. The relationship between practitioner and client was viewed to be more important than any specific technique used (McKeel 1999). This finding is similar to the Lambert (1992) study that shows how important relationships are in working to promote change. One specific study was from a parental support group (McKeel 1999). When asked the miracle question all 12 parents were able to answer, with most reporting that this made them feel 'more hopeful about their situation'. Other studies in the review reported increased hope following the miracle question as it encouraged them to 'focus on their goals . . . and helped them focus on doing something different to accomplish their goals'.

These results are very positive and provide a sound rationale for adopting solution focused skills.

One factor raised by examining effectiveness is how little we seem to ask ourselves and parents what helps. This can be asked during the meeting, at the end of the meeting or in a follow-up at some later date. After meetings we often can go into problem mode and think of all the things that went wrong. This is the time to think about exceptions and what did help so that they can be used in the future. It is really only by asking the parents that we will discover more about how we can be even more effective.

## Getting started and continuing to develop SFBT skills

Perhaps the best place is to start with our goals and some scaling questions:

- Where are you now in the viewing and doing of SFBT? Use a scale of 0–10 where 0 is I am very new to this way of working and not yet tried it and 10 is SFBT is my way of working. Where are you now on the scale?
- Think about your goals; what would you like to achieve? How can you make your goals well formed? Where would you like to be on the scale?
- What would help you to reach the next point on the scale?
- Think of something you have learnt in the past, for example swimming, playing an instrument or learning a language. What helped your learning? Was it watching someone else, reading a book or regular practice? How could you use these strategies to be successful with SFBT?
- Motivation to learn is an important aspect. On a scale of 0–10, how motivated are you to work in a solution focused way where 0 is not at all motivated and 10 is 100 per cent motivated? What might increase your motivation?
- What else would help develop your skills?

Some other options are:

- Record meetings by either tape or video to review what helped. This provides an opportunity to think about the other questions that might have been asked. Of course permission from parents is essential and with some words of explanation, 'I want to make sure I didn't miss anything' (De Jong 2000).
- Use the start small principle. Experiment with one aspect of SFBT, for example exceptions, building cooperation, using the placebo factor, scaling. See what works.
- Find out if there are other people interested in developing these skills and solution build together.
- Share your successes with your school and help create an environment where solutions are key.

## Summary

This chapter is an introduction to what SFBT has to offer, from a way to viewing things that are challenging for us and for the effective techniques which create cooperative interactions. Viewing and doing things differently are called for when working together with parents where there are behavioural issues. This can be a challenging and emotional time for everyone involved. It is therefore critical that we work in ways that work.

SFBT offers a framework that utilises the key factors for successful intervention – client factors, relationship factors, placebo factors and model factors, and research has shown it to be effective.

## References

Ajmal, Y. and Rees, I. (2001) *Solutions in Schools*. London: BT Press.

De Jong, P. (2000) *How to Improve Your S-F Skills. More research needed.* Online: http://www.brief-therapy.org

de Shazer, S. (1985) *Keys to Solution in Brief Therapy*. New York: Norton.

de Shazer, S. (1991) *Putting Difference to Work*. New York: Norton.

de Shazer, S. (1994) *Words Were Originally Magic*. New York: Norton.

de Shazer, S. (1996) *Creating Change*. Two-day conference, London. Organised by Brief Therapy Practice, London.

Department for Education and Employment (DfEE) (2000) *SEN Code of Practice on the Identification and Assessment of Pupils with Special Educational Needs*. Consultation Document. London: The Stationery Office.

Durrant, M. (1993) *Creative Strategies for School Problems*. Eastwood Family Therapy Centre, Australia. Alexandria, NSW: Bell Graphics.

Gillies, E. (2000) 'Developing consultation partnerships', *Educational Psychology in Practice*, **16**(1), 31–7.

Gingerich, W. J. and Eisengart, S. (2000) 'Solution-focused brief therapy: a review of the outcome research', *Family Process* **39**, 477–98.

Lambert, M. J. (1992). 'Implications of outcome research for psychotherapy integration', in Norcross, J. C. and Goldfried, M. R. (eds) *Handbook of Psychotherapy Integration*. New York: Basic Books.

McKeel, A. J. (1999) *Solution Focused Therapy: a selected review of research of solution-focused brief therapy*. Online: http://www.enabling.org

Murphy, J. J. (2000) *Solution Focused Intervention for School Problems*. International Presentation. Cardiff.

Murphy, J. J. and Duncan, B. L. (1997) *Brief Intervention for School Problems: Collaborating for school problems*. New York: Guildford Press.

O'Hanlon, B. (1999) *Do One Thing Different*. New York: William Morrow and Company.

Rhodes, J. and Ajmal, Y. (1995) *Solution-Focused Thinking in Schools*. London: BT Press.

Stephenson, M. and Johal-Smith, H. (2001) 'Discovering the Expert', in Ajmal, Y. and Rees, I. (eds) *Solutions in Schools*, 188–201. London: BT Press.

Wagner, P. and Gillies, E. (2001) 'Consultation: a solution-focused approach', in Ajmal, Y. and Rees, I. (eds) *Solutions in Schools*, 147–62. London: BT Press.

Wolfendale, S. (1997) *Working with Parents of SEN Children After the Code of Practice*. London: David Fulton Publishers.

# CHAPTER 12

# The Best Chance of Success

If the child does not respond readily to the concerted efforts of home and school, then . . . both home and school will need to draw on the established partnership in their efforts to find a solution. If this partnership is not established early parents may feel they are being blamed for their children's difficulties and may avoid contact with the school, damaging the potential for working together.

(DfE 1994: paragraph 15)

## Introduction

Nearly a generation ago the Elton Report (DES 1989) in Britain focused on improving relationships between home and school as a way of addressing disruptive behaviour. Schools were encouraged to take active steps to break down barriers between schools and families. Recommendations included:

- ensuring that positive and constructive comments on pupils' work and behaviour were sent home regularly
- encouraging parental involvement in the classroom
- involving parents at an early stage of behavioural difficulty
- providing a welcoming and accessible environment for parents
- encouraging good home–school communication going beyond formal channels
- ensuring that written communications were easily understood by the parents
- ensuring that behavioural policies were communicated fully and clearly to parents.

The concern about behaviour in schools has continued unabated since the Elton Report, along with much discussion about what to do about it. Working in collaboration with parents/carers would still appear to offer

the best chance of success and the above recommendations are reinforced both by the views of parents quoted here and by the contributing authors.

Knowing *what* to do, however, does not seem to be enough. Unless sufficient attention is paid to *how* to put good ideas into practice they stay at
the theoretical level. Positive home–school interaction for behaviour is
potentially very fruitful but requires certain perspectives to get off the
ground and a high level of skill to maintain. Whether this is seen as a priority for school development is closely bound up with school culture.

Many examples of good practice are illustrated here. There are both
schools and individual teachers who strive to establish and maintain good
relationships with families and take positive action on behalf of children.
The outcomes are not only for individual pupils, but also strongly related
to school effectiveness (Rutter *et al.* 1979, Mortimer *et al.* 1988, Sammons
*et al.* 1995). What might be queried is why this good practice is not
reflected everywhere.

## Choices in perspective

People think and talk about issues in different ways and some perspectives are more useful than others. This is illustrated by the anecdotal stories
in Chapter 1 and reinforced throughout this book. The social discourse in
a school – the conversations that take place – can reinforce the prevailing
views of families and of children. Challenging an unhelpful but prevailing
discourse requires courage, skill and effective leadership. Individual teachers may develop their own good practice and although this has positive
outcomes at the time, it does not necessarily give children or parents a
consistently positive experience. Once that teacher is no longer on the
scene there may be disappointment, frustration and deterioration in behaviour. It is the culture within the whole school that determines the eventual outcome.

The two interrelated conceptual strands of school responsibility and the
place of parents determine the extent to which collaborative home–school
partnerships to address behaviour can be established within a school.
These perspectives are on a continuum and most schools are at a point
along the way. What is important is the direction in which they are moving.

### School responsibility

Where schools promote an inclusive environment in reality as well as in
rhetoric they are more likely to take responsibility for all children and

respond positively, flexibly and creatively to individual differences. This entails all children being welcomed and accepted and their difficulties being viewed from a needs perspective as well as a management one. Schools that accept that they are responsible for effective responses to distressed and disaffected pupils acknowledge that what they do may exacerbate as well as modify student behaviour. Such schools take proactive measures to teach behavioural expectations and include pupils who are vulnerable, do not jump to conclusions about attribution, prioritise relationship and communication skills, have positive behaviour policies and only exclude pupils when they have exhausted all other options.

This perspective is of particular importance when it comes to prevention, early intervention and children's early experiences in school. What happens in those first early school experiences is critical if children are to have a sense of belonging, maintain motivation and not think of themselves as failures in the system. Many behavioural difficulties can at least be modified with appropriate intervention. The earlier this happens, the better. The indications here are that many behavioural difficulties are related to learning needs and self-esteem issues, experiences of loss leading to confused and/or angry feelings, poor social skills or lack of understanding about expectations. Although there are some young people who have had very damaging life experiences or have specific neurological disorders and will eventually require intensive support, these are in the minority. Most of the time positive early intervention can make a difference. Working in partnership with parents can make a significant difference.

## Partnership with parents

School perspectives on children affect how parents are viewed and the possibilities for active collaboration. Blaming the family, either directly or covertly, for the child's behaviour and handing them the entire responsibility for 'doing something about it' is the opposite of a partnership perspective. Parents who are seen as having complementary expertise and whose ideas about their children are elicited and taken into account when planning can be effective partners in joint interventions. Where the principles of partnership are not in place, parents either 'fight' to achieve a more equitable power balance, develop sophisticated skills to try to 'work the system' or opt out altogether.

## Principles into practice

### Communication

All the messages given in schools by formal and informal means communicate to parents how they and their children are perceived and valued. This includes what information is given and how, the ways in which meetings are organised to facilitate participation, the interpersonal and professional skills of teachers and the ability to deal constructively with conflict and confrontation. There are also issues about within-school communications. The most crucial communication skill is the ability to listen. Solution focused approaches outlined in Chapter 11 by Elizabeth Gillies outlines ways of listening to parents to elicit their competencies and ideas for solutions.

### The whole child

Parents usually want their children to be accepted as complete individuals. They may admit the existence of difficult behaviour but often want this to be seen in context of other concerns. They respond most positively to teachers who try to share their perspective on the child and mirror their parenting priorities. Some parents are aware that they lack expertise and may be looking for guidance. This is most effective when it is developed in a shared framework rather than imposed by 'experts'. What happens in a child's first educational provision or when difficulties are first identified is critical.

> *'I'm single and I work and I've got no family. I found it quite difficult because you just don't know if you're doing the right thing. You feel so desperately alone.'*

Parents, especially those who are struggling, need support not labelling. This is illustrated in Chapter 7 when Anna Harskamp talks about working effectively with families who harm their children and keeping the ultimate needs of the child in focus.

Where families are not able to fulfil one or more of the parenting functions of acceptance, care, protection, encouragement and socialisation it is even more important that schools do so *in loco parentis*. Although teachers are not there to be parents, schools can either reinforce negative experiences for children or they can go some way to compensating for them.

## *The whole family*

Sometimes parents are simply overwhelmed with other concerns in their lives. Acknowledging these makes it possible for everyone to be realistic about the possibilities. Mobile families are often in this category and Anthea Wormington in Chapter 9 illustrates how schools need to take account of home circumstances both for parents and for children. Parents may also have very different expectations and interpretations of situations based on their own experiences and cultural norms. It is unrealistic to expect teachers to know individual circumstances but schools do need to find ways that limit misinterpretation and are responsive to parents' own concerns. Ann Phoenix highlights the need for more research on this in her chapter on diverse communities (Chapter 10).

## Initial training and professional development

Up to now there has been surprisingly little attention paid to how teachers might work more closely and effectively with parents on behavioural issues, especially at early stages. Dialogue with parents, especially those who may appear angry, defensive or apathetic, requires both a perspective and a competence that does not necessarily come naturally. Teachers need support to maintain a professional stance at all times and avoid taking behavioural issues in school personally. As well as training in interactive processes it would be helpful for teachers to understand different ways of construing behaviour and the interactions between systems that may be involved. This needs to include the impact of loss for children and the importance of early intervention. This would also be helpful for professional carers as mentioned in Jean Law's chapter on children in public care (Chapter 8).

## Summary

The aim here has been to highlight what works, to identify good practice and to focus on what helps parents, children and teachers feel better about their experiences in school. All of this has far-reaching implications for training, management, organisation, priorities, allocation of resources, expectations, communication structures and school culture. There are particular implications for the use of time.

The search for answers to the problem of pupils who are hard to manage in school is likely to continue. There is no one solution but we do have to make choices. Either we focus resources on early identification and intervention, finding ways to work as positively as possible with parents, or we will be obliged to fund the effects of social exclusion where the outcomes are potentially devastating, both for individuals and for society as a whole.

Teachers have a hard job to do. They have many demands on them, for high academic standards, to maintain good discipline and to meet individual needs. Teachers who find themselves in the firing line, criticised by all and sundry, may have a struggle to maintain their own motivation. Schools need the support, resources, professional development and encouragement to help them respond in ways that we know are more effective. Attainment targets are important in education but so is the whole child and every child. Losing sight of this is a detriment to the future.

## References

Department for Education (DfE) (1994) *The Education of Children with Emotional and Behavioural Difficulties.* Circular 56/94. London: The Stationery Office.

Department of Education and Science (DES) (1989) *Discipline in Schools: Report of the Committee of Inquiry.* Chairman Lord Elton. London: HMSO.

Mortimer, P. *et al.* (1988) *School Matters: The junior years.* Taunton: Open Books.

Rutter, M. *et al.* (1979) *Fifteen Thousand Hours.* Wells: Open Books.

Sammons, P. *et al.* (1995) *Key Characteristics of Effective Schools.* London: OFSTED and London University Institute of Education.

# Index